PHOTOSHOP 7 PROFESSIONAL PHOTOGRAPHIC TECHNIQUES

JANEE ARONOFF
NYREE COSTELLO
GAVIN CROMHOUT
VIKAS SHAH

friendsof

DESIGNER TO DESIGNER™

an Apress™ company

ISBN 978-1-59059-147-5   ISBN 978-1-4302-0779-5 (eBook)
DOI 10.1007/978-1-4302-0779-5

Printed and bound in the United States of America
2345678910

Trademarked names may appear in this book. Rather than use a trademark symbol with every occurrence of a trademarked name, we use the names only in an editorial fashion and to the benefit of the trademark owner, with no intention of infringement of the trademark.

Distributed to the book trade in the United States by Springer-Verlag New York, Inc., 175 Fifth Avenue, New York, NY, 10010 and outside the United States by Springer-Verlag GmbH & Co. KG, Tiergartenstr. 17,69112 Heidelberg, Germany.

In the United States: phone 1-800-SPRINGER, email orders@springer-ny.com or visit http://www.springer-ny.com
Outside the United States: fax +49 6221 345229, email orders@springer.de or visit http://www.springer.de

For information on translations, please contact Apress directly at 2560 Ninth Street, Suite 219, Berkeley, CA 94710. Phone 510-549-5930, fax 510-549-5939, email info@apress.com or visit http://www.apress.com

The information in this book is distributed on an "as is" basis, without warranty. Although every precaution has been taken in the preparation of this work, neither the author(s) nor Apress shall have any liability to any person or entity with respect to any loss or damage caused or alleged to be caused directly or indirectly by the information contained in this work.

The source code for this book is available to readers at http://www.friendsofed.com in the Download Center.

Credits

Authors
Janee Aronoff
Nyree Costello
Gavin Cromhout
Vikas Shah

Commissioning Editors
Adam Juniper
Luke Harvey

Editor
Julie Closs

Author Agent
Mel Jehs

Project Managers
Simon Brand
Jenni Harvey

Technical Reviewers
Terry Boedeker
Darlene Billmair
Dan Caylor
Steve Voisin
Josh Fallon
Steph Ridlet
Alexandra Blackburn

Indexer
Fiona Murry

Proofing
Victoria Blackburn
Caroline Robeson

Graphic Editor
Matt Clark

Cover Designer
Katy Freer

Managing Editor
Chris Hindley

CONTENTS

Gavin Cromhout lives in Cape Town, South Africa, where he works as a new media designer and digital photographer. He learnt most of what he knows about photography from carrying around his grandfather's camera case as akid. This was known as being a photographic assistant apparently.

His past book contributions include:
New Masters of Photoshop
DigitalPhotography with Photoshop Elements
Photoshop Face to Face.

You can reach him via his company
website: www.lodestone.co.za or drop him an email: gavin@lodestone.co.za.

Janee Aronoff was born ... wait... you know that already! You want to know who I am now and what I can do for YOU, right?

If, indeed, we are what we have done, I'm a lot of things! Long before I discovered Photoshop, I was a student and a teacher, working with my tenth graders to explore high school geometry through creating art. My Master's thesis was on the building of polyhedral solids to teach 3D visualization. What that meant was that my classes were often working with crayons, glue, and scissors!

After several years, I left teaching and opened a small bakery. Then wedding cakes became my canvas! When I decided to take my business online, I discovered, instead, that I love doing digital art. I bought Photoshop and a tablet, the learning-and-teaching fire was rekindled, and here we are!

From my home office in the woods near Bloomington, Indiana, USA, I now operate a flourishing Photoshop resource website at http://www.myjanee.com. Here I maintain my collection of tutorials, links, and Janeefacts.

I have spent much of my life nurturing thoughts that I had to "do my best" and that "perfect is not good enough." I now believe that perfectionism and negative thinking are twin demons which prevent us from discovering the artists within ourselves. The goal is not perfection. The goal is DOING!

I also believe that art springs from vision. And since no one else has YOUR vision, no one else can do YOUR art!
Always me, Janee

Nyree Costello has been a professional photographer for the past seven years. Having trained as a photojournalist, and prior to branching out on her own, she worked at an Ontario newspaper for two of those years. Simultaneously, she taught photography at a local arts center to teens and adults looking to expand on their creative knowledge.

Since she grew out of news photography she has kept something of a photojournalistic approach in all of her images. She now owns her own photography business - where the majority of her work is done for modeling and talent agencies. She also offers wedding photography in her off beat style and sells artistic pieces at private galleries.

In addition to this, Nyree contracts out graphic/web design services to private companies and organizations. She became a self-taught web designer after she baulked at professional offers to build her company site. Deciding that she could do a better job, she the plunge into the high-tech world.

Her photography experience works in a synergistic manner with her design skills making for some unique high-energy creations! You can view her work at www.photosbynyree.com.

Vikas is chairman and CEO of Ultima Group, a leading multi-award winning design agency, established 1994, based in Manchester, with clients worldwide including Nike, Unilever, The Queen's Golden Jubilee (String of Pearls Festival) and Sage Software. He is also an accomplished designer and manager, holding an associateship at the UK institute of Management since he was 19 and having won a semi finalist position in the Ernst & Young Entrepreneur of the Year awards. Vikas regularly lectures and speaks at schools, universities and events around the country as well as writing for magazines and other publications. He is also an accomplished photographer and digital artist, having co-founded egoRush.com, a UK based digital arts project which received over 1.3million visits in its first month online. Vikas also consults and advises with many advertising & design agencies as a creative director, advising on design practice and innovative strategy.

Introduction

Photoshop is the industry standard photographic program. Whether you want to improve your photos with a bit of color correction, restore old pictures that have been damaged, or create new work based on your favorite photographic images, Photoshop is the program for you.

What's more, the latest version, Photoshop 7, has more techniques available to you than ever before, in terms of new tools to facilitate your photographic work. The Healing brush, in particular, is covered in detail within these pages and can be a revelation to even the most hardened graphics expert. That said, you will find a multitude of techniques to achieve professional level results with your images that will work with an earlier version.

This book is designed to help you get the most out of this fantastic program, by taking your photographic work to new heights. We'll show you the tricks of the trade, and how to maximize the usefulness of Photoshop to achieve stunning results.

You may be coming to this book via any of several paths. Perhaps you are a professional photographer making the move into a digital workflow. We'll show you how to recreate those traditional darkroom effects, without the chemicals and costs, so that your creativity can run wild. Maybe you're a digital artist looking to improve your skillset when it comes to photos. We'll let you know how the pros handle the tricky tasks, like turning less than perfect shots into polished images. And perhaps you're an enthusiast, looking to achieve those professional effects seen in magazines. We'll show you how the professionals work, so that you too can take advantage of the amazing possibilities that come about when you harness the power of Photoshop.

Platform specifics

Photoshop users are as likely to be Mac-based as they are to be Windows-based, and for this reason, screenshots are relevant to both platforms. Throughout the book, you will see a mixture of Mac and Windows screenshots. Regardless of this, any keyboard shortcuts will be written with the Windows one first, for example:

CTRL/⌘-C translates as pressing the CTRL (CONTROL) button and tapping the C button in Windows, or pressing COMMAND (⌘) and C in Mac OS.
CTRL/⌘-SHIFT-C means Ctrl & Shift & C in Windows or ⌘ & Shift & C in Mac OS.

All about this book

As stated earlier, the book is eleven chapters long, each chapter standing independently and focusing on a particular aspect of photographic work within Photoshop, such as restoration and retouching, or color correction.

The sections are more about practice than theory, but we do begin each with an introduction telling you what we will be focusing on in the exercises. Where necessary, we've provided a bit more background information, to ensure you have the know-how and confidence to take the techniques examined further, into your own work.

Every chapter has three or more exercises, showing you, step by step, how to recreate the effects shown. And if you are interested more in one area than another, the chapters stand independently, so you can go straight to what you need to know, rather than working through the whole book in order.

We do assume basic knowledge of the tools in Photoshop, but no more than that. We have also provided the images for you to download at www.friendsofed.com. It's probably easier to follow the exercises using these, but you may prefer to use images of your own where you need to tackle similar problems.

To keep things as simple as possible we've only used a few layout styles to avoid confusion.

At the start of each exercise you will see a box like this, containing a before and an after illustration, for guidance, and a bulleted list of tools that are used in the exercise.

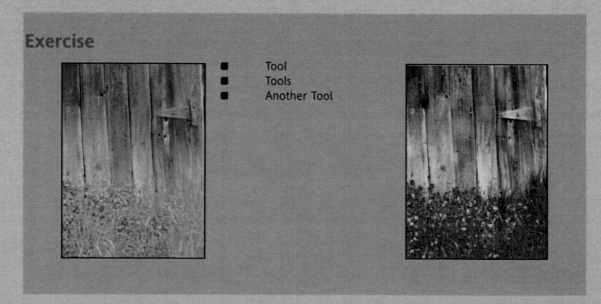

Exercise

- Tool
- Tools
- Another Tool

In the time-honored fashion we have numbered the steps of each tutorial, like this:

1. Do this
2. Then do this
3. Do this next, etc...

Sometimes we'll draw your attention to an important word or tool with bold type, especially if it is the first time a concept is discussed:

In this chapter we'll learn about **Non-Destructive** Editing...

We've used different fonts to highlight filenames, and URLs too:

waterhole.psd and friendsofed.com

All our menu commands are given in the following way:

Image > Adjustments > Hue/Saturation

This equates to the following action on your screen:

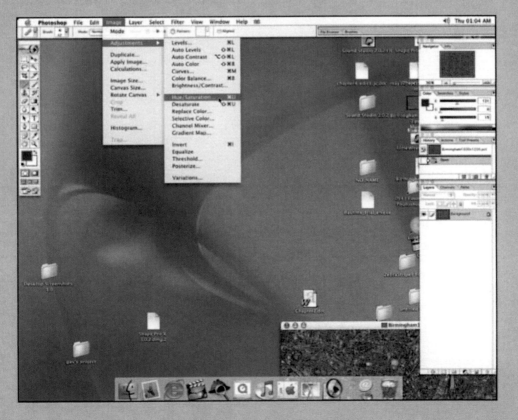

Finally, throughout the book, you may come across boxes with information inside them.

> *If the box looks like this, this means the information contained is important for you to note, and worth remembering outside the context of the specific example. It may be a helpful tip or a warning about what you are doing, etc.*

Hymn sheet

This text assumes a basic familiarity with both your computer and the Photoshop interface. Just to be sure we're all singing from the same hymn sheet, here are the terms we'll be using for the assorted parts of that interface:

We have used all the standard Adobe names for the tools in Photoshop 7. For the most part they should be familiar with any other reference material you use, including the built in help. We've noticed, however, that a lot of people seem confused by the name of the Clone Stamp tool, for example – you may know it as the Rubber Stamp, or simply Clone.

Files for download

To produce the results as shown, you can download the source files required for the exercises from our web site at www.friendsofed.com and click on the 'Downloads' page.

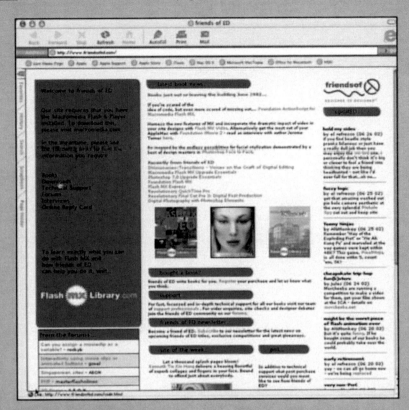

On the site you'll also find a host of other features that may interest you – interviews with top designers, samples from our other books, and a message board where you can post your questions, discussions, and answers. Or you can take a back seat and just see what other designers are talking about.

Support

If you have any technical queries about the book, you can mail support@friendsofed.com for a quick response. If you have any more general or non-urgent queries or comments, you can mail us on feedback@friendsofed.com. We'll answer all mails quickly and efficiently. If you have anything you'd like to talk to us about, please contact us. We'd love to hear from you.

Chapter 1
Color and Calibration

Understanding color

Quick, think of a color. Not a particularly difficult task is it? But how about thinking of a color that no one else would think of. Now that sounds a bit more tricky! However, it's not actually that hard. Before I tell you why, let's get a better understanding of color.

Color theory is fundamental to all our work in Photoshop. Although it may sound like a bit of a dull, or scientific topic, it is crucial that we understand how color works so that we can appreciate how our images are perceived.

Basically, it all comes down to light. At the risk of stating the obvious, without light, we would not be able to see anything. Whether we are looking at light waves directly, or indirectly when they are reflected off objects, all the color, texture and shading we see is controlled by the way our eyes process light.

In this chapter, we will be looking at how we perceive color, and the difference between additive color, (observing light directly) and subtractive color, (where the color we see depends on what is reflected from the image surface).

From here, we will move on to gaining an understanding of the RGB and CMYK color models, and how these are used in our Photoshop work. We will also take a look at the concepts of hue, saturation and brightness, and gamuts and how they affect our workflow. We'll look at some of the less-used color modes in Photoshop, and finally examine how we can manage color at every stage of our image process to get the best possible match between the captured scene, and the final result, whether displayed on screen or in print.

1

The foundations of Photoshop lie deeply embedded in color theory, so we'd better take a closer look at it. Any discussion about color should start with ourselves – after all it is our eyes that take in the information and process it so that we perceive color.

Why tennis balls are not yellow

You've probably heard the start of the old philosophical argument, "If a tree falls in the woods and no one is around…". Along similar lines it's interesting to note that objects themselves have no color without us seeing them – our own eyes and brains simply interpret the way light is reflected off things. This is *our* interpretation and not something necessarily intrinsic to the objects themselves.

The little cells in our eyes, called cones due to their shape, contain various chemicals, which enable them to distinguish between different wavelengths of light. They come in three flavors – one interprets certain wavelengths as blue, another identifies others as red, and the third kind translates light into the color green. These sensors are active together in varying percentages, so we are able to blend these colors together to see pretty much any color – a spectrum of around 5 million colors, in fact! So, that's why tennis balls aren't yellow: they aren't actually any color at all. Our eyes and brains simply interpret the wavelengths of the light bouncing off them.

But what about learning in art classes that the primary colors were red, blue, and yellow? First tennis balls aren't yellow, and now we find out that yellow doesn't even rate being a primary color anymore? The point to remember here is that light and paint combine in very different ways. For example, if you mix red and green paint together you get brown, but if you mix red and green light together you get yellow.

How can this be? Surely color is color no matter how we use it? Well, not quite. Anyone who's messed around with paint will tell you that unless you're using white, the more paint you mix together, the darker your mixture gets.

I remember learning in science classes that white light is formed from the entire spectrum of colors. So basically the *more* colors we throw together in light, the brighter and whiter the resultant light will be. In terms of the RGB color we use in Photoshop, (made up of light rather than paint) this can be seen in the fact that R:255, G:255, B:255 makes up the brightest white we can get on our computer screens.

Additive and subtractive color

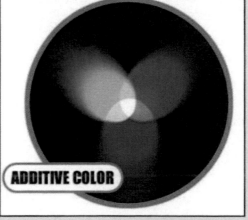

ADDITIVE COLOR

Combining color in this way is called **additive** color – we add them all together to make white. Our eyes, as we have seen, use this system to create different colors. With paint, it's just the opposite. So in theory if we wanted to get white in paint, we'd have to remove all the colors. Another way of looking at this is: Red paint is red because it traps a certain wavelength of light and reflects the rest. Our eyes interpret this wavelength as red. So the more paint that's added means the more colors / wavelengths that are trapped. This absorption (**taking away**) of wavelengths is called **subtractive** color.

Colors don't stand alone either – they are interactive. For every color there's an opposite color – a negative color. How does this work? Let's say you stare at a blue object for some time (in excess of 20 seconds). This means that the cones in your eyes that interpret this wavelength of light are doing a lot of work. Now if you stare at a piece of white paper, *all* the cones of the eyes have to record the color (remember white is the total additive color), but the cones that were doing all the work on the blue are now tired, and hence cannot do their work as well. Consequently they can't contribute properly to make the color white in your brain, so what happens is the red and green receptors end up making the image. Now as we know, red and green, when combined as light, make yellow. So basically, if you stare at a blue object for long enough then look away, you see a yellow afterimage.

Let's try this out, just to check, and because it's cool! Stare at the image opposite for more than 20 seconds, and then when your eyes are watering and the edges are starting to glow, look at a completely white piece of paper. After a few seconds you should see an after image appear, in the complimentary colors to those shown opposite.

If you combine two of the primary additive colors (red, green, or blue), the resultant color is one of the primary subtractive colors (not quite red, blue, and yellow, they are actually *magenta, cyan,* and yellow). Basically, the three primary subtractive colors are formed from the colors that are left when you remove a primary additive color. So staring at blue gives you yellow, staring at red gives you cyan, and staring at green gives you magenta. They are therefore complementary colors – when combined they cancel each other out. So subtracting blue means that two additive colors are left (red and green) which your eye will add together to give you yellow. If you therefore mixed these three primary subtractive colors, you'd also get white light.

1

Why, what beautiful cones you have!

Looking at this in another way: red, green, and blue are the three colors that our eyes use to interpret the different lengths of wavelengths of light. If you combine all three, you get white light. If however you stare at something too long, it's quite easy to temporarily wear out the cones that handle one of the three wavelengths. Actually, fixing your eyes on an object means you wear all the cones out to a lesser or greater degree, depending on what colors are present, but for the purposes of our discussion let's just say you wear out the blue ones. You're lying on your back, staring up at a whole lotta blue... Wearing out one wavelength receptor (group of cones) means the remaining two (red and green) are left to try and make up the image by themselves. So when everything is mushed together, the left over colors combine – in this case to form yellow. Performing the same task, but fixating on a *different* primary color would yield different results, in the form of either magenta or cyan. So these three new colors (cyan, magenta, and yellow), which as you can imagine could also create white light if combined, form the primary **subtractive** colors – *removing* them from the spectrum would yield a primary **additive** color.

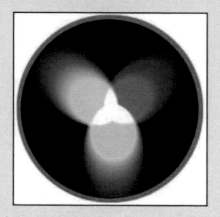

In the above image we can see how any two of the primary subtractive colors can combine to form white light – this is because any one of them is formed from TWO primary additive colors: So combining yellow (a mixture of red and green) with magenta (a mixture of red and blue) gives us red + green + red + blue – a bit of overkill, but white light nonetheless!

Previously we were discussing how paint and other objects trap certain wavelengths of light on their surface, which is what our eyes interpret as color.

Just as no two sets of fingerprints are quite the same, no two sets of eyes are quite the same. Studies have shown that although most people perceive red as being red (for instance), because of the unique morphology of our eyes, it is possible that we all interpret the identical wavelength of a particular object slightly differently. With colorblind people these differences are extreme – a completely different interpretation of the wavelengths of light to most people. With the rest of us, the variations are almost impossible to detect, but in all likelihood present nonetheless. So there you go – picking a color that no one else is thinking of is probably not that difficult after all!

Computer screens use light to display color, and therefore use the additive color system to make color. This system is often known as the RGB (red, green, and blue) color model.

The RGB color model

We've already discussed how red, green, and blue light combines to form white light. This method of combining colors to form brighter and lighter colors uses an *additive* process. Additive colors are used for lighting, video, computer screens, and digital cameras.

The RGB mode

There are obviously lots of different ways of displaying color on a computer monitor. Photoshop makes use of the RGB mode by default, which is a system based on the RGB color model we have just described.

Basically Photoshop assigns intensity, ranging from 0 (black) to 255 (white), to each pixel, the color of which is made up by combining red, green, and blue. Let's have a look at a few colors created this way:

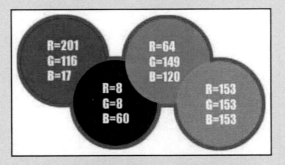

The first color, ochre, has a lot of red, about half as much green and very little blue. Remember if we'd had equal amounts of red and green we'd have yellow. But because we have more red, the color tends towards orange.

The navy blue we've used for the second color has very little of every color, but is strongest in blue. Because each color is much closer to 0 than to 255, we get a very dark color as the result.

Our third color, which is a kind of sea-green, has significantly higher amounts of green and blue, which, combined, give us cyan. Because of the fairly mid range percentages of each of these colors, we end up with a kind of teal/dark sea-green color.

Our final color has equal percentages of each color, which gives us a perfect gray. Obviously as the percentages of

1

each color get closer together, the more the colors cancel each other out, and the less saturated the resultant color will be. Remember when we combine all three primary additive colors at their full strength, 255, we get white.

If we now combine a slightly weaker set of lights – say at 80% each – the colors still cancel each other out perfectly, but because the intensity of each isn't enough to make white, you get a light gray. If we'd combined 5% of each, we'd still cancel out all the colors, and end up with a really dark gray. Isn't this great? The next time you're at a tennis match, you can now stand up and shout: "Hey, nice R=222, G=254, B=3 tennis ball you have there!" Or.... not.

The only difficult thing about using the RGB model is that it's not exactly intuitive. It's hard enough trying to picture red and green combining to make yellow, but what about turquoise and brown? Well obviously we don't have to work out the percentages of each color – Photoshop does all this for us, all we have to do is use the Color Picker.

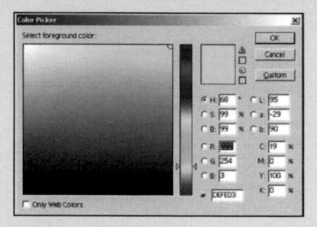

Notice the color slider just to the right of the main color area. At the top and bottom we have red, and evenly spaced between we have blue and green. Notice how between red and blue we have magenta and between blue and green we have cyan, etc. Clearly we are sticking to the RGB color model here.

Take the blue channel

You can also see the RGB color model at work when you're in RGB mode by looking at your Channels palette.

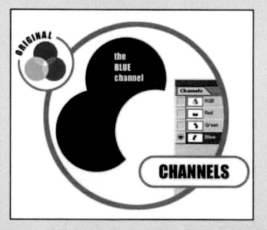

As we can see from the above image, if we just show the blue channel in the Channels palette everything that contains blue (the white background, the magenta and cyan slivers, and the big blue circle) is shown up as white – meaning these areas have blue in them. The black parts (the primary red and green circles and the yellow sliver) contain no blue, and are therefore depicted with black.

The HSB model

Basically the slider in the color picker starts and ends with red because it is a linear representation of a spherical color chart. Instead of just having our three additive primary colors, we now have a chart with the entire spectrum:

Hue and Saturation

Have a look at the image of the color picker again. Notice there are three extra fields above the R, G, and B value boxes labeled H, S, and B. These stand for hue, saturation, and brightness.

We've just mentioned that the slider on the Color Picker dialog box is a linear representation of the above spherical chart. Basically the H (the hue) is a number from 0 at the bottom (0° on our chart, being the red to the left of the H), to 360 (actually labeled correctly as 0 again which is 360° anti-clockwise around our chart back to the same red).

The next value box down from the H is the S which stands for saturation, and is illustrated on the above color chart as the distance along the line represented by S. This is a value from 0% to 100%, where 0% is completely gray, and 100% is total saturation.

Finally we have the B value box, which as we know stands for brightness. Values range from 0% (pitch black) to 100% (the full-bright color).

RANGE OF COLOR

BRIGHTNESS

1

Although we won't directly be using this color model, as in Photoshop there is no HSB mode available for creating and using images, it's a useful reference when adjusting values in a dialog box. Keep it in the back of your head, along with the RGB values of the tennis ball.

So now, when you look at a Hue/Saturation dialog box, you have a greater understanding of what's going on.

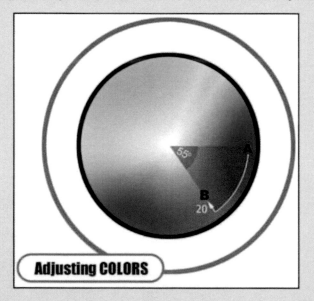

In the previous image we saw two color strips at the bottom showing you, in a linear fashion, how we're going around the color wheel. Notice how the top strip (which represents the original color, A) is now out of alignment with the bottom one (the new color, B).

We can note that we've gone 55° around the color wheel to a magenta color (shown by the Hue setting of -55) and then desaturated slightly by traveling towards the center of the wheel, (shown by the Saturation value of -20):

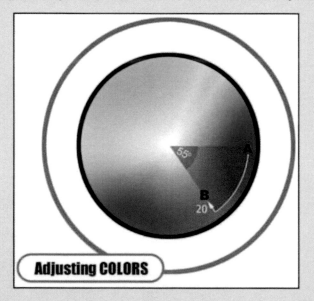

Adjusting COLORS

The CMYK color model

As opposed to the light-emitting additive RGB color model, the CMYK color model is based on the **light-absorbing** qualities that objects have. Instead of making something *brighter* when you combine colors (which would be additive), combining colors with this model makes things darker, as more is absorbed. Looking at this in another way: the fewer colors we have, the lighter the combined color becomes. The CMYK color model therefore uses the **subtractive** color process.

These primary colors we have seen to be Cyan (C), Magenta (M) and Yellow (Y). In theory, if we combine these colors we get black. But if you've ever tried this, or had an early Hewlett Packard color inkjet, you'll know that what you *actually* get is a muddy dark brown.

The reason for this is that impurities exist in ink and paint that prevent you from getting a true black. For this reason we cheat a little and just add some black paint / ink ourselves. We use the letter K to denote black – it stands for Key.

the CMYK color model

So instead of having three channels, we now have four. Remember how when we added together cyan and magenta light to produce white light we had: red + green + red + blue, and we noted that we had more colors than were necessary (two reds). This was fine because we already had white light without the one red, so adding more light is just overkill. The same principle applies here.

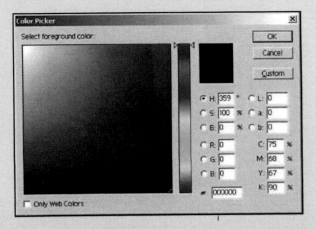

1

Notice that even though we've selected pure black (from the bottom right hand corner) and the RGB values are all zero, the K (black) value (at the bottom right) is only at 90%. This is because we have already achieved pure black by mixing the colors together.

The CMYK mode

In CMYK mode, color is expressed in terms of percentages, this time of each of the *four* process colors. Although many professional printers these days are able to print in RGB color mode, most still require CMYK. This means that you will have to convert your RGB image to CMYK. By using **Image > Mode** this task is easy to accomplish, but notice that the entire color of the image changes slightly. Usually the image becomes a bit darker. Because we changed from one color model to another, a conversion has been made. Remember that we are now going to be using a different set of colors to create the image. This leads nicely into a whole new range of problems...

Gamut

As we mentioned earlier, the RGB color model uses a combination of red, green, and blue to create white light. With this method we can create almost all colors in the spectrum of light. But almost is the operative word here – even with this method, not **all** colors can be created this way.

For instance, we cannot see the near and far ends of our own color spectrum – infrared and ultraviolet. This is because our eyes do not possess the right kind of cones to respond to these wavelengths of light.

In a similar kind of way, monitors cannot display the entire range (called a **gamut**) of colors that our eyes can see. The CMYK gamut is even smaller than the RGB one, comprised only of colors that can be printed using process-color inks – which, as you can imagine, is more limiting that the kind of colors we can create just mixing light. When colors that cannot be printed are displayed on the screen, they are referred to as 'out of gamut' colors (out of range colors). These colors are therefore those that fall outside the CMYK gamut. This is only something you need to take into account for printing really, which isn't the focus of this book, but it is something to be aware of.

Gamut warnings

Photoshop has a few handy ways of warning you when you step outside the bounds of safety with the color picker. If you try to select a color in RGB mode in the Color palette, you will see an exclamation mark appear with a small box showing the nearest CMYK color.

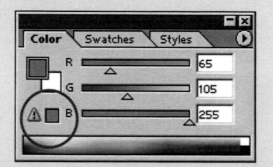

If you move your pointer over an area of the image with a color that falls outside the CMYK gamut, the Info palette will reveal that with the subtle addition of an exclamation point at the end of the CMYK color values.

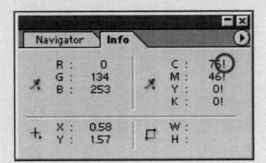

You can also get your computer to highlight the areas of your image where that exclamation point would appear. A quick glance tells us that this snap of Copenhagen is over-saturated, but it's hard to judge exactly where there would be serious problems.

Clicking **View > Gamut Warning** (CTRL/⌘-SHIFT-Y) shades in all the areas outside the gamut you have chosen (**View > Proof Setup** to change from the working CMYK default). In this case, all those shocking roof tiles, and even the Danish flag in the foreground have all been highlighted.

Other color modes

Photoshop doesn't just use RGB and CMYK color modes, there are in fact quite a few that can actually be used.

Grayscale mode

This mode works along similar lines to the RGB color mode – except it uses 256 shades of gray. This mode would be used where you scan something in from a scanner that doesn't have color, for instance. You can convert an image from RGB to grayscale to remove color: **Image > Mode > Grayscale**. Or you can do the opposite and convert a grayscale image to color – not that this will make the image color, mind you, but it will allow you to add color should you now choose to do so.

So what is the use of this mode? Twofold: Firstly we use it when an image is in black and white – because it has been scanned in that way. We can then convert from this mode into whichever color model takes our fancy. Secondly, if we want to make an image duotone (consisting of two main tones) like an old photograph – we first need to remove all the color from the image, and we do this by going via the grayscale mode.

Indexed color mode

This mode is far more restricted than the RGB color model, using at most 256 colors. So this color mode uses a color lookup table, which stores and indexes the colors in the image in order of luminosity. When converting to this mode, if a color in the original image does not appear in the table, the program chooses the closest possible match or combines available colors to simulate it (usually using a pattern).

By severely reducing the palette of colors, an indexed color image can be much smaller than other modes as regards file size while still presenting a fairly high quality image. This is especially evident in images with large areas of flat color. Why? Imagine the RGB file (an example of which being a .tif file) looks something like this: color 143 color 543 color 143 color 143 color 219 color 16 etc. Let's say we had a huge block of red. The RGB file would look something like: color 16 color 16 color 16 color 16 color 16 etc. As you can see it's rather boring talking to areas of flat color, and I don't recommend it. I don't even think your tennis ball joke would go down well...

But with an indexed color file you would get: color 16 for the next 23 pixels. Saves a lot of space doesn't it? This makes the file size a lot smaller. Because of this, multimedia applications and web pages make extensive use of this color mode.

However the fairly restrictive nature of this color mode means that many of the editing options will not be available for use – so do your editing in RGB color mode and then convert to Indexed when you're done.

LAB color mode

This is probably the least well-known and most disused color mode. This is not to say that this color mode is useless, however. The LAB color mode is designed to be **device independent**. This means that reliably accurate color can be created regardless of the device used to create (such as a camera or a computer screen) or even duplicate (such as a printer) the image.

This mode has three components: L (Lightness), ranging from 0 to 100, and two color components. They are the A (colors ranging from red to green) and the B (the remaining colors ranging from blue to yellow), using the same HSB color wheel we have used previously.

Because your computer screen uses the RGB color model, many of the LAB colors cannot actually be displayed. This model was used to circumscribe accurate color *independent of device* remember, and this includes your computer screen.

The basic use for this mode is a kind of transition mode when you convert from one color mode to another. Photoshop will first convert to LAB color (just because the colors can't be displayed doesn't mean they can't be mathematically calculated), and then adopt the new color mode you have chosen.

Match-making

The process of taking a photograph and displaying it is a fairly complex one as far as color is concerned. If you're using a conventional analog camera, you will need to create prints of the photographs and scan these in. Already, in the background, a lot of color conversion has taken place:

Firstly, the photographic film of the camera has captured the light, using a chemical process. The film is then developed – which means the light altered chemicals on the film are used to produce a permanent change on photographic paper. So light is converted into ink. It's quite possible at this point that already discrepancies exist between the color of the original scene, and the photograph.

These are of three main sources:

- Poor quality film, or the wrong film.

- Poor photography – using the wrong shutter speed and/or the wrong aperture for the lens for instance will produce results that will not mimic the original subject matter accurately. Often this is intentional, but let's say this is our task: to accurately reproduce the colors of different flowers.

- Poor development– using the wrong combination of chemicals, the incorrect amount of chemicals, or leaving the chemicals for too long or short a time can also drastically alter the accuracy of the color in the image.

At this point we will need to scan the photograph in. Once again, a conversion process is being made – from ink back to light. Depending on the scanner, color inaccuracies could also be introduced at this stage.

Only now, after many color changes, do we have the image in its 'raw' state. Once we have added some design we will need to prepare the image for its final output. Web preparation means that color variation may be something sacrificed for the sake of file size, and if your image is destined for print, it will probably have to be converted back into printer friendly CMYK color mode. Without changing anything, it's almost certain that yet another shift in the overall color will be introduced at this point.

And that's not the end of it. How your image displays on your audience's screens will depend on browser and monitor capabilities and settings. And if it is being printed, the printer will now have to interpret the file and convert the pixels into patterns of ink. A lengthy road as far as color is concerned.

1

There are a number of steps we can take to try and minimize these possible inaccuracies. A while back we talked about every person having different eyes, and therefore interpreting color in a slightly different way. This is also the case with computer monitors. Luckily, it's slightly easier to rectify this.

There are two main tasks that can ensure better color accuracy: calibrating the gamma, and setting the ICC color profiles.

Orange you glad you red this far?

Calibrating the gamma sounds like something involving truck spanners and strobe lights. Luckily it's not that difficult to accomplish (no spanners are actually involved). So what is gamma anyway?

Basically the gamma is the brightness of the midtone values between black and white. You'd expect the tones produced from black to white to be linear in fashion, but this is not the case, they actually exist along a curve – largely because of the design of most computer monitors. The gamma value defines the slope of that curve halfway between black and white.

So not only do we mess up the color by just getting the image to our screens, the major problem may exist in the way our computer screens actually display the color. And of course, our original problem still persists: Just about everyone has a different type of monitor, a different type of graphics card (the piece of hardware inside the computer responsible for sending an image to the screen) and all sorts of (ever changing) display drivers (the software responsible for getting the graphics card to do anything in the first place).

In order to avoid more of a color tangle, we use ICC (International Color Consortium) profiles. Each pixel in our image has a color. This color is created using a color mode – probably the RGB color mode, which means numbers are used to create a certain resultant color.

But how the computer interprets these numbers and uses the hardware to display the color on the pixels is quite a process. ICC color profiles standardize this process so that discrepancies in hardware and software are taken out of the loop.

Getting pernickety

So what is the best way of accurately reproducing color? Well the best way is to drag the person that wants to see the different flowers out to the spot that you found them. Obviously this can be tricky, and to some extent time consuming. If for example you want to take pictures of the flowers for a calendar, you'd have to make many trips – at least one a month, with hosts of different people. I'm not knocking this method per se, but let's for the time being explore other avenues.

Let's go with the runner-up system of ensuring the correct use of color.

Yay or Nay

Firstly, is it necessary to use a color management system?

A color management system looks at how a color was created and then looks at how it will be used. If there is a discrepancy, the system makes the necessary adjustments to try and maintain a level of consistency across devices. Although this can maintain consistency of color, the color itself isn't corrected. This is your job! All this system will do is allow us to accurately view how badly we've managed to take that photograph after all. So is it useful?

Well if you're using many different types of devices (scanners, computers, printers, and so on) from different manufacturers, color management helps you accurately reuse color images. So if you were using lots of workstations to complete your projects, for instance, unifying everything using a color management system would be advisable.

However, as most people who publish to the web know, you cannot control the color settings on the monitors of all the people viewing your website (for the same reason as outlined in our calendar problem: many people would take exception to you pitching up at their homes to calibrate their hardware, every time they clicked on your website). The best we can hope for is using Web Graphics Defaults settings, which at least uses the most popular RGB color systems out there.

Some inroads are being made into this problem through the .PNG file format, which embeds a color profile – but as this increases the file size it has yet to truly break into the web scene. Anyway, to change and use your color management, use **Edit > Color Setting**s. We will go into this in slightly greater detail in the final chapter when we look at preparing your images for publishing.

Keeping it real

Color management can only go so far. But there are other steps we can take to try and ensure the original color ends up in the final product:

- When viewing your images, try to be in an area with consistent lighting. The sun has this nasty habit of moving around a lot – which changes both the amount and color of the light. So keep the shades closed when you want to evaluate the color in your images. Fluorescent lights don't exactly give you good color either. Even though they're consistent, they tend to add a rather greenish hue to things. You can get 'daylight' bulbs, which are a lot better, but at a price.

- The interior of the office is also important – try and keep the color of the walls and ceiling fairly neutral (unlike my office, which looks like a Rubik's cube). And if you're prone to wearing luminous green t-shirts, this might just mess up the colors you see on the screen by its reflection on the monitor glass.

- So if you've smashed your neon light and are now sitting in the (gray walled) filing room wearing a black raincoat, you're probably off to a good start. Probably not with your colleagues however.

- Also, try get the amount of light in the room similar to that from your monitor – an excessively bright room will make the colors on the screen look falsely dark, while a really dark room will make them shine out too much.
- When you're viewing images on your desktop, maximize them so that nothing else can be seen, including all your palettes (the Tab key will toggle this).

- Finally, and this is a really important point, try to view your document proofs in the real world. Print the stuff out and take it to where it's going to be used. It's all very well to get all this color matching right only to find the stuff is going to be used in a factory that has mainly neon light bulbs.

All this color theory may seem like a bit of a bore, but it really can make the difference between amateurish and professional quality photographs.

Chapter 2
Color Correction

Color correction is perhaps the easiest thing to learn and the hardest thing to master. Easy to learn because Photoshop lets you see what you're doing before you're committed, hard to master because it's so subjective. Professionals will tell you that, after years working in the field, there is no right answer for any one photo, but there are plenty of wrong ones!

In the last chapter we learnt a little of the theory behind color – what it is, how we see it ,and how we represent it in Photoshop. When we considered how the brain coldly interprets wavelengths as the visible spectrum, we were only looking at the scientific side of the story. The brain also *interprets* what it sees, translating the patterns of light into a picture of the subject – a pretty girl, a bridge, whatever.

When you look at an object in real life, your eyes concentrate on it and the brain makes subconscious color corrections that make the subject appear natural. This is easy for the brain, of course, because it knows what you're looking at, and your eyes pick up a higher 'resolution' on the target of your gaze. Your camera doesn't think and understand, so it sees the whole image evenly.

This means that, in many cases, we can correct an image by choosing the subject and making some quick adjustments that bring it to life, and consider other elements of the image secondary. Sadly, it isn't always quite that easy. The brain is capable of other tricks. For example, if your friend has put a red sock in the washing machine, hasn't mentioned it to you, and is wearing a shirt that you expect to be white then – so long as the color the shirt has picked up is very mild – you might still see that shirt as white.

The same effect can happen to any number of colorcasts made by lighting environments and, again, the camera isn't intelligent enough to be fooled like this. This leaves you with a bit of a moral dilemma: Given that the colors the camera has captured are quite possibly more accurate measures of the original colors, but not the ones we'd expect, should we change our image at all?

The answer is easy if your image is for a client. It is, of course, whatever they want. It would be fair to say that the solution should normally be to make the image seem right to the viewer, which would mean removing the colorcast, however natural it is. That said, if you wanted to humiliate the victim of careless washing machine use you'd want to leave, or enhance, the shade!

Colorcasts

Before we get ahead of ourselves, we first need to know how to identify colorcasts. This is a skill that will improve the more you do it, so don't give up if you have some trouble identifying the colorcasts at first.

Below are some very easy ones. Each has only one, strong colorcast so that you can learn to recognize each color. For purity purposes, the image used is black and white. Refer to these images as guides to help recognize what colors are in your image that need correcting.

2

MAGENTA

GREEN

YELLOW

BLUE

CYAN   **RED**

2

Take a good look at the magenta and red images. Note the differences in the hues. Magenta has a light pink look to it and red, well, looks more like red. When you are correcting an image and are not sure if the colorcast is magenta or red, more times than not it's magenta. So when you are correcting an image always try correcting for magenta first unless you are sure it's red. You can have both magenta and red in an image, if this is the case then correct for the most obvious colorcast first. Then move on to the next obvious cast. As you are doing this you may find that you have to go back and re-correct for a color as more casts are eliminated.

The same problems occur with blue and cyan. These two can be easily mixed up if you don't know what to look for in the image. Cyan has more of an aqua tone to it and tends to hide in the shadows and highlights of an image rather than displaying an overall cast – this isn't to say that it won't though. Blue is more likely to completely cast over an image and sometimes has a blue-purple feel to it. It is possible, as well, to have both blue and cyan in an image.

Yellow and green are fairly easy to distinguish between. But when combined with other casts, they are sometimes mistaken for each other. A good rule of thumb is that if there is magenta in the image, then it's yellow you are seeing. Another way I distinguish subtle yellow colorcasts from green colorcasts in an image is that yellow gives a warm feeling to an image. Green, I find, just makes a picture look muddied. Remember though, it is possible to have both yellow and green in the image.

Color correction is made by adding the colorcast's complementary color to cancel it out. They are as follows: magenta and green, yellow and blue, cyan and red.

Armed with this information we now know that magenta and green are used to cancel each other out, as do yellow and blue; and cyan and red. What does this mean, you ask? Well put into application, if your image has too much green in it (a green cast) you would need to increase the magenta amount to reduce the green. The same goes if for example you have too much yellow in the image. You would increase the amount of its complementary color, blue, to eliminate it.

One point you should note that will help make the task of identifying colors easier is that there can only be three of the above colorcasts in an image at any time – as there can not be any two complementary colors in the image at the same time. Since we use magenta to cancel out green in an image, there can't possibly be too much green and magenta at the same time. The same goes for yellow & blue, and red & cyan.

There can be red, yellow, and green, but never red, yellow, and cyan as red and cyan are complementary colors and cancel each other out. So if you have an image that you think you see magenta and some green, what you are really seeing is magenta and some yellow perhaps combined with some cyan.

Along with correcting for the colorcasts, an important part of the process is correcting for densities. The most common tools to do this are Levels, Curves, and Brightness/Contrast. We are going to use each of these methods to correct different images so you can get a feel for each one. You choose which one you like the best.

Correcting the density of an image is an important step in the color correcting process and must be done first so that we know exactly what color we are correcting for. If an image is too light or too dark, we may end up over-correcting for a colorcast or correcting for the wrong color altogether.

Keep in mind that, despite Photoshop's excellent tools for correcting density, there is no substitution for a properly exposed image. If you are trying to balance out a severely under or over-exposed image, Photoshop is the program for you, but it will take some knowledge and work on your part.

With that said, Photoshop does offer a few different ways to do this in the Adjustments options under the Image menu. These options can be applied directly to an image or with an Adjustment Layer. You'll find that the more you use Photoshop, the more ways you'll discover to complete a task. In this chapter we will go through each of the density-correcting options to show the difference in how they are used and how they, in the end, achieve the same thing.

Don't bail out on me now! It's really not as difficult as it sounds. Let's just dive right in.

(Remember you can download the files to follow along from www.friendsofed.com).

Using levels and color balance

- Levels
- Brightness/Contrast
- Color Balance

2

Let's start with the easiest and most user-friendly method – Levels. Levels are a way to modify the color in an image by adjusting its tonal range and individual color channels. The histogram displays the image data for the full range of tones – highlights, midtones, and shadows. (The term histogram is used to describe the graph that shows the pixels at each level of brightness.)

1. Open up girl.tif.

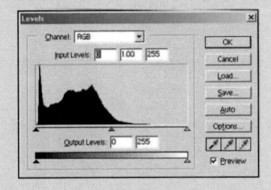

2. Duplicate the 'Background' layer and re-name it 'Girl'. Turn the visibility of the Background Layer off.

The histogram, represented by spikes on the graph, shows the number of pixels in the image that have that corresponding value. With this in mind, when we are correcting using Levels the aim is to have a rounded curve where the arc is highest in the midtone range (middle of histogram).

3. Choose **Image** > **Adjustments** > **Levels** or CTRL/⌘-L on the keyboard.

Take a look at the histogram for our image and get familiar with the interface. The triangle Input sliders on the bottom of the histogram are used to represent shadows, midtones, and highlights respectively from left to right. As you move these, the numeric Input Levels display the gamma values. If you enter in a value, the sliders will move accordingly.

Along the bottom are the Output Levels. The left slider is for Output shadows and the right is for Output highlights. This makes the entire image darker or lighter by modifying the gamma values from the image.

Look at the graph. Right now the arc is to the left of the midtones, which is represented by the middle slider. As mentioned above, we want the arc to be in the midtones.

4. Use the highlight slider (on right) and drag it to the left until it reaches the beginning of the arc. Drag the shadow slider (far left) to the right slightly until it is on the arc as well.

2

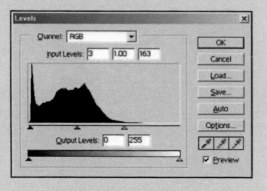

What we have done is taken the highlights, which were not displayed at all in this dark image, and modified the gamma for it. By moving the highlight slider over to register on the graph we have brightened the image. Take a look at the image to see the effect.

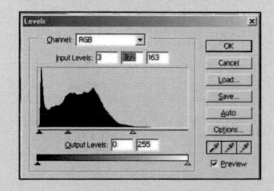

5. The image has brightened up quite a bit, but it's still pretty dark in the midtones – especially in the subject's face. To lighten this up more, we are now going to drag the midtone slider over to the left until the image is brighter, but not washed out. The slider should rest in the middle of the rounded arc.

Click OK and take a look at the image now. By modifying the midtones we have improved the image's overall

brightness. We can now see that we have to correct for some magenta.

Before we start correcting for the magenta we are going to do one last step in correcting the density. The image is much better than when we started out, but it is still a little flat.

> When we refer to an image as being "flat", we mean that the image lacks contrast. The opposite, too much contrast, might be called "too punchy".

6. To remedy this choose **Image > Adjustments > Brightness/Contrast**. Set the Brightness to 15 and the Contrast to 15 as well.

Now we are ready to start correcting for the magenta in the image. How did I know it was magenta? As I mentioned earlier in the chapter, magenta creates a pink cast on an image. How dark the cast is varies with the amount present. In this image, there isn't too much.

As I mentioned already, one of the great things about Photoshop is that there is always more than one way to carry out a task. This is also true with color correction. For this image we are going to use Color Balance to remove any magenta from the image. Color Balance, located in the Adjustments submenu, let's adjust the colorcasts in an image by using sliders for each set of complementary colors.

7. Go **Image** > **Adjustments** > **Color Balance** or CTRL/⌘-B on your keyboard.

Leave the Tone Balance option set to Midtones and drag the Magenta/Green slider to the right only far enough to get rid of the magenta but not so far as to start adding green. Make sure you have the Preview option checked so you can see the effect in your image.

Now take a look at the image.

Yikes! Where did that yellow come from? One of the things you'll discover when doing color corrections is that sometimes there is more color there to correct then you think. In this case, the magenta in the image hid the slight yellow cast that is also there.

8. To get rid of the yellow, drag the Yellow/Blue slider over to the right again only so far as to remove the yellow but not so far as to add any blue. Look at your image as you are doing this. You'll know if you've gone to far as the image will have "cool feel" to it. (When an image has too much blue or cyan in it, we refer to it as being "cool". Conversely, if an image has too much yellow, we refer to it as

being "warm".)

That's better. Our image is now set at a proper density and the colors look great. Take a look at the corrected image in comparison to the original image. What a difference!

2

Using curves and variations

- Curves
- Variations
- Brightness

2

Now we are going to correct another image using a different technique – Curves. Curves, much like Levels, adjust the tonal range of an image, but allow for pinpoint control over the entire color spectrum. With Curves you can be as general as you would like or as specific as going in to modify each color channel. Using Curves requires a little more skill and the basic understanding of color values and channel separations as it is not as forgiving of mistakes as Levels is.

That said, once you have this understanding, Curves is the most effective and powerful tool in the color correction process. To simplify using this option remember this: To brighten an image, click on a point in the line and create a curve where the arc is sloped to the right. To darken an image, create a curve where the arc is sloped to the left. (This is based on the brightness portion of the bar put on the left side. If the brightness is on the right the opposite is true.)

1. Open `fenced_flowers.tif`. Duplicate the 'Background' layer and rename if 'Fence'. Turn the visibility of the 'Background' layer off.

Now take a look at the image. It's very easy to see that the image has some magenta in it, but let's correct the density before making any guesses.

2. Open Curves by choosing **Image > Adjustments > Curves** or by pressing CTRL/⌘-M on the keyboard.

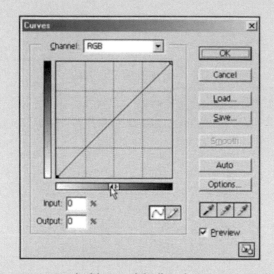

We are presented with a straight line that represents the gamma. When the line is straight it indicates no change in contrast. We need to darken this image as it's a little washed out.

3. First make sure that you have the brightness bar set to the left side of the graph by clicking on the arrows in the middle of it.

4. Now we are going to create our curve. To do this, click in the middle of the line to create a point. Drag this point to the left moving slightly upwards creating a curve like the one below:

Wow that was easy. As I mentioned, Curves is a very powerful tool in Photoshop but one that many people avoid as it is a little daunting. However, in the right hands – yours – it is a very fast and effective way to correct the tonal balance in an image.

Well now we are ready to start our color correction. Begin, as always, by making note of the colors we are going to correct for. The image is very warm – this means that the colorcasts are on the warmer end of the spectrum, such as magenta, yellow, and red. The Magenta cast is obvious and a colorcast I find I correct for the most. I also see a bit of yellow as well. What do you see?

For the color correction, this time around we are going to use Variations. Variations allows you to see the colors as you are adding them, and as with other techniques you can set the adjustments to affect the saturation, highlights, midtones, or shadows portions of the image. The difference is that you see the image in the window, rather than having a preview option. While performing corrections using Variations, you can, at any time return to the original image by clicking on the Original image box.

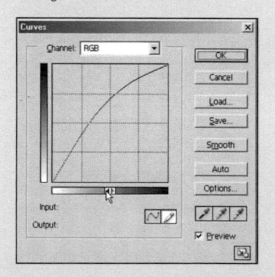

As you create the curve the image darkened, but the contrast also increased. Take a look below.

2

5. Choose **Image > Adjustments > Variations**.

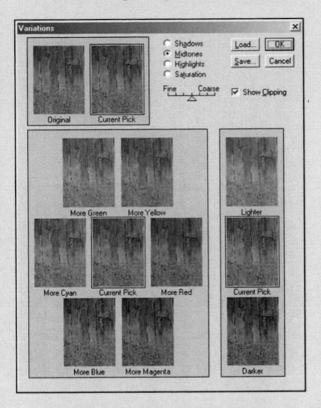

As we discussed in the beginning of this chapter, to get rid of a color we have to add its opposite to cancel it out – magenta's opposite is green on the color chart, so to correct for magenta we have to add green. To get rid of the yellow, we have to add blue.

Make sure the tonal balance is set to midtones and that the Fine/Coarse slider is set to the middle of the scale as shown in the image above.

6. Start correcting for magenta, which is the most predominant color here. To do this, click on the more green image and look at the Current Pick image. Did we get all of the magenta? I'd say yes. If you had the Fine/Coarse slider towards the Fine end we would have to add green a few more times to eliminate all the magenta cast as it would be applied more lightly to the image.

7. Take a look at the image. Do you see the yellow now? It's more apparent now that we've corrected the magenta. Now let's correct for it by adding blue. Click on the More blue image to add some blue to the image. I think that did it. Click OK.

If you are correcting for a slight yellow colorcast but find that the image was too blue when you added one click of More blue, you could set the Fine/Coarse slider towards the Fine end of the scale to lighten the application of the correcting color.

Now take a look at this image that has been corrected for both magenta and yellow. Not bad.

It looks good, but I think it's still a little warm. Since we have already corrected for magenta and yellow, the only other warm color is red. If you look in the fence you can see a slightly reddish hue. I see this right away as I took the picture and know what color the fence originally was. You will do this as well when you are correcting your own images. With that said, if you are correcting an image and it looks different from the actual subject but you like it better – feel free to use your artistic license! There are no rules here.

In the case of this image, I don't want it to look quite so warm. I really want to show the weathered look of the wood.

8. Open up Variations again by choosing **Image > Adjustments > Variations**.

9. Hold down the ALT/OPT key to turn the Cancel button into a Reset button and reset the palette. By resetting the palette we are working off the color correction for the new version of our image. Now correct for the red by adding a shot of cyan to the image.

10. It's a bit too much isn't it? Reset the palette again. This time move the Fine/Coarse slider one increment left to lighten the application of the cyan. Add the shot of cyan again.

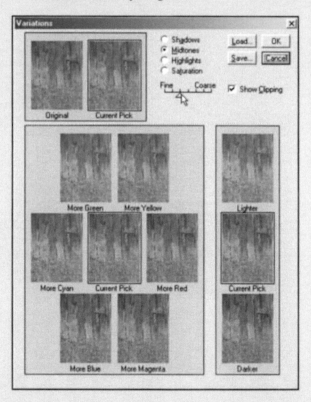

11. Again look at the Current Pick. In the highlights of the wood I still see some red. Switch over to the tone balance for Highlights and put the Fine/Coarse slider back to the middle. Add another shot of cyan to the image.

2

12. Our color looks much better. You can now really see the weathered look of the wood. The image, however, is still looking a little flat. So let's finish it off by adding some contrast. Go **Image > Adjustments > Brightness/Contrast**. Leave the Brightness set to 0 and change the Contrast to 20.

Brightness/Contrast	☒
Brightness: 0	OK
	Cancel
Contrast: 20	☑ Preview

Congratulations, you've done it!

2

Separate curves

- RGB Curves
- Levels

This photo of Toronto has beautiful picture postcard composition but sadly the smog has given the image something of a pinky cast. What we want to do is give it the same rich perfect blue sky as a postcard without turning the buildings blue. Using Curves we can achieve that without the effort of selecting any specific areas of the image.

1.   Create a Curves Adjustment layer.

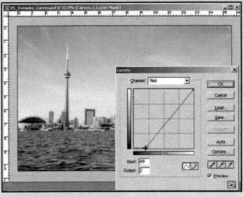

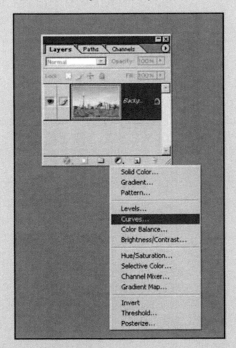

3.   Drag the bottom left marker in a little, which moves the dark tones (represented by the vertical axis) in a lighter direction.

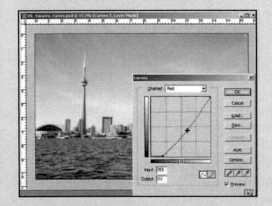

By clicking on the line, we can drag it to the right a little, reducing the strength of the red midtones.

2.   Looking at the image, the first thing we need to do is tone down the red shades, especially at the darker end because the water is definitely a little too red. Using the drop-down menu at the top, select the Red curve.

37

2

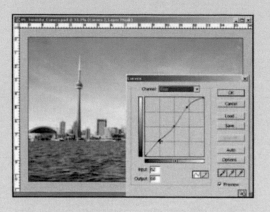

6. Create a new Levels Adjustment layer above the Curves adjustment and use the markers to adjust the contrast to your liking.

If you find the histogram has an unnatural look-ing shape – lots of thin spikes rather than a soft-er curve – this is probably because there has already been some processing on it. This is why it helps to have a perfect original – the processes in Photoshop are mathematical and there are only so many colors. A lot of processing can reduce the number of shades you are using.

4. Moving on to the blue, there is a need to strength-en the tones, especially at the lighter end of the scale (the tones that affect the sky). A slightly more complex curve, created by clicking and dragging in more than one spot, easily does the trick.

Our final image, possibly with a sharpen filter (**Filters > Sharpen > Sharpen**) applied, looks much more like a picture postcard, without adversely affecting the tones of the city itself. In our heart of hearts, it's probably the blue we always want to see so we don't have much trou-ble believing it.

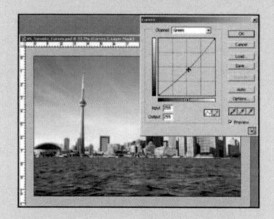

5. Finally we need to make a minor reduction of the green tones with our simplest curve yet – a little movement can make a big difference.

All our changes have left the image in need of a little more contrast. Again, this is easily fixed.

2

Automatic corrections

- Auto Levels
- Auto Color

2

Finally we are on the last exercise for density and color correction. Here we are going to use the Auto Levels option and Photoshop 7's new Auto Color feature to correct an image and to also show how accurate it can really be.

Auto Levels works like Levels, except you are letting Photoshop determine what the tonal values should be. You loose the ability to tweak the tone towards target areas as Auto Levels takes into consideration the entire image. For the most part it does a pretty good job, there are some that are best corrected using manual Levels or Curves. Personally, I'd rather have the control over what is adjusted in the image and therefore stick to manual Levels and Curves.

Auto Color automatically makes color adjustments by reading the tonal and gamma values and makes corrections accordingly.

1. Open `sky.tif`. As usual, duplicate the 'Background' layer and rename it 'Sky'. Turn the visibility of the 'Background' layer off.

2. Choose **Image > Adjustments > Auto Levels** and take a look at the image.

Not too bad, the foreground is a little darker than I'd like it to be, but it works in this image and I can live with it if need be.

Now we are going to correct the color in this image using Auto Color. Before we apply this, take a moment to note the colorcasts in the image. If you look in the cloudless portions of the sky you can see that there is magenta to correct for.

3. Now apply the Auto Color by choosing **Image > Adjustments > Auto Color**, and let's see if the program saw the magenta too.

It did. It's magic I tell you! We could, at this point, leave the image as it is. I did mention that I could live with the foreground if need be, but luckily I don't have to. So let's brighten up the foreground a little to show some detail.

4. Select the Polygonal Lasso tool and set the Feather to 3px. The reason we set a bit of a feather on this tool is to avoid having the foreground look like it's been cut out after we brighten it up. By feathering the selection the two areas are blended together.

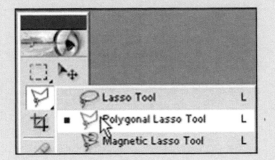

2

Curves if you don't want to use one. Click in the middle of the line to create a point and slowly drag the line to the left until the image has brightened slightly. Your curve should look similar to the one below.

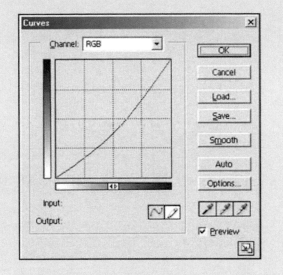

5. Now select the foreground of the image. It should look similar to the image below.

6. Let's try applying the Auto Levels again to this selected area to see how it does. Go **Image > Adjustments > Auto Levels**.

9. Deselect all by pressing CTRL/⌘-D on the keyboard and take a look at the final image.

7. Yuck! It looks so pixelated. This is definitely a task that will be better accomplished by adjusting the tonal values manually. Go back a step in the History palette or by pressing CTRL/⌘-Z on your keyboard.

8. Let's try this again, this time using Curves. Either create an Adjustment layer for Curves by selecting the icon located at the bottom of the Layers palette or by choosing **Image > Adjustments >**

41

2

2

Chapter 3
Adding and Subtracting
Features from your Images

The perfect photo is rarely, if ever, captured. There is often something annoying in the background, or the sky is not clear. Perhaps someone didn't make it into the group photo, or an employee at the company has been replaced. Maybe we want to take a candid shot and transform it into a portrait. Sometimes we want to create the impossible, whether placing our subject into the clouds, placing a car under a toadstool, or "building" a house in the Grand Canyon. Are these insurmountable problems? Not if we have Photoshop!

In this chapter, we will explore some techniques for removing objects from photos, adding people to photos, and changing parts of photos. Along the way, we will discuss some of the problems inherent to this sort of work, how to prevent them, and how to solve them.

We will be covering several varied examples of the sorts of things you may wish to do, but every photo will present its own unique problems. The example we use may present a completely different situation in regards to light and shadow, for example, than your particular problem photo does.

There are boundless opportunities for creativity in your ideas and in your expression of them. In these examples we will be exploring just a tiny bit of what can be done with these photos. I hope that you will use the ideas presented here merely as a springboard for your own creativity!

3

Peggy's Cove lighthouse

- Clone Stamp tool
- Patch tool
- Transform
- Photo composition
- Layer masks

This is a nice photograph of a Nova Scotia Lighthouse. There are a few things that we can change, though, to make it even more beautiful. First, let's crop this photo to make the lighthouse come into the foreground. Next, let's get rid of all of the tourists. Finally, we can clear the sky.

Protect your work

Before changing anything in the photo, it is a good idea to do a bit of preliminary backup work in order to protect your images. First, save the file with a new name. This way, if you botch the job badly, you can always return to your original picture. Save it into .psd format and please, every time you accomplish anything you like, hit CTRL/⌘-S to save. Don't let a power burp at the end of a long day wipe out your day's work!

Here is one more little "backup" maneuver to carry out before we continue: Duplicate your image layer. This can save you considerable time if you mess up your working layer. Drag it to the New Layer icon in the Layers palette. Then turn off the eye for the bottom of the two layers to make it invisible.

Cropping the photo

Let's begin by cropping the photo to lose some of the foreground rock and a bit of the sky. Type C to bring up the Crop tool, drag out your rectangle, and then adjust it. Click ENTER to crop.

Removing people by cloning and patching

Next, we will take the people out of the picture, and while we are there, let's remove that trash can. With Photoshop, there are at least three different ways to do anything:

- If your offending person is isolated in the scene, you can often do well with the Patch tool or the Healing Brush tool.

- If your unwanted person is against more than one different background color, the Healing Brush tool or Patch tool may yield unsatisfactory results. For the people in this example, because of the variation in the background, you are likely to do better using the Clone Stamp tool.

First we will do some cloning.

Using the Clone Stamp tool to remove people from the photo

1. Make a new layer by clicking the New Layer icon at the bottom of the Layers palette.
    Rename it 'cloned-out people'.

    Let's first get rid of that person in white to the right of the lighthouse. Since she is against two different distinct backgrounds, this is a good time to use the Clone Stamp tool:

2. Select the Clone Stamp tool in the toolbar, and make sure **Aligned** and **Use All Layers** are checked in the options bar.

3. Choose a brush size. For this, we want a pretty small brush, because we will be zooming in tightly.

4. We need to select a source, which we will use to paint out the figure. Hold the tool over a bit of blue sky near to the person we want to remove, as shown on the next page. Hold down the ALT/OPT key and your tool becomes a sampling tool with crosshairs. Click your mouse to select your sample.

5. Then release your ALT/OPT key, go to your destination, your offending person in this case, and paint her away!

3

Aligned *keeps the same distance between your destination and your sampled area, so that your source point moves along with your brush, no matter how many strokes you make. When this is not checked, when you release your brush and begin to paint again, the source reverts to the original spot.*

Use All Layers *enables you to clone onto the new blank layer. If this were NOT checked, if you tried to clone onto this blank layer, your source would also be blank, and so nothing would happen!*

3

When we get over to the large group of people on the left, our task is a bit more complex, because we have to guess what the rocks behind them might look like.

6. Take a sample from one of the rocks near to the people, shown by the green ring in the screenshot below. Sample, then clone.

7. Then grab another sample from a similar, but different, area, then clone. In the yellow ring, the sample was taken more closely to the cloning. This sort of work takes a bit of practice

In cloning, one problem that we can encounter is an effect called "patterning." This occurs when you don't take a new sample, but keep on painting with new strokes. So be careful to sample often, and from differ-

ent areas as you go. Here is an example of the sort of regularity that we do NOT want!

So here is our picture as it stands so far:

Removing people with the Patch tool

This fellow to the right looks pretty alone now, doesn't he? Well let's magic him away, too. He is a good example of a gentleman who could be removed with Photoshop 7's Patch Tool. To use the Patch tool, your blemish, in this case, the man, must be against a pretty plain background. This figure's immediate background is a fairly simple collection of granite boulders.

Let's try the patch:

1. Choose the Patch tool in the toolbar. It is under the Healing Brush tool.

2. Check **Destination** in the options bar. Draw around your destination — where you want your patch to end up. In this case, it will be around our man.

3. Now you need to specify your source. Click **Source** in the options bar and then with the Patch tool within your selection, move this selection to where you want your patch to sample.

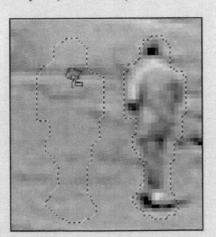

Ta-da! Our landscape is patched! The tourist is gone!

Up to the sky!

Though I've seen worse days, a clearer sky would be a better complement to the lighthouse. There are many ways to accomplish this, but essentially, we want to make a selection of the sky, either delete it or hide it, and then make (or find) a sky to put in its place.

Selecting the sky

The method(s) you use for your selection will depend heavily upon the level of contrast between your background and your subject, upon how busy the background is, and upon the shapes involved.

This example is well suited for a combination of methods, actually. Since there is quite a demarcation between our subject and the sky, at least for part of the border, we might choose the Magnetic Lasso tool to start.

1. Choose the Magnetic Lasso tool (under the regular Lasso) in the toolbar.

2. Set Feather to 0 px, Anti-aliased checked, Width of 10 px, Edge Contrast 10%, and Frequency 50.

3. Make your selection loosely around the border between the scene and the sky. Don't worry if it doesn't select it perfectly. Enclose the part of the image that you want to keep, not the sky.

4. Double-clicking your lasso, at any point, will finish your selection by connecting where you click with your starting point.

Since the selection is not perfect, we can touch it up, still using selection tools. The straight Lasso tool is often good for this.

5. Hold the SHIFT key as you add more parts that you want to keep into your selection. If there is an area you want to subtract from your selection, hold the ALT/OPT key as you drag the lasso around these. Zoom in so that you get a close look at this.

Notice that you get a little + or − depending upon whether you are adding to or subtracting from your selection!

Hiding the sky

Once we have the selection pretty close to where we want it, adding a Layer mask will hide the sky, but leaving it in place, so that we can always return to edit it further.

Click the Add Layer Mask button at the bottom of the Layers palette. And there goes your sky! Notice when you add the mask, you will get a tiny mask that appears beside your layer in the Layers palette. The black parts of the mask hide their pixels, and the white parts show their pixels.

If you want to make sure that you get all the "fringe" pixels, it is often helpful to put a black, a white, and a midtone gray background layer beneath your masked layer. In this way, you can more easily see the out-lying pixels.

If you do have corrections to make, click on the mask in the Layers palette. Your image won't look any different, but the little brush in the Layers palette beside the eye changes into a little mask icon. This indicates that you are about to work on the mask. Choose your paintbrush and use black or white, depending upon whether you want to show more pixels or hide more. (Gray in the layer mask will make the pixels semi-opaque.)

Replacing the sky

Now we can add the weather of our choice. It is sometimes difficult to pick out a good "sky blue," because the sky's blueness varies with place and time.

1. If, as in this case, there is some blue in the sky, it will serve you well to select that blue with your Eyedropper tool and use it as a starting point for your sky gradient. To see your sky again, right-click on the mask you made for the lighthouse. Choose Disable Mask. Make your color selection and then double-click your mask to hide that sky again.

4. Now this sky is a little too pristine, so let's add some wispy clouds. This can be done on a new layer with a subtle application of a white 45-pixel airbrush at 50% flow. Then some judicious Smudge tool work will finish it off realistically, blending your wispy clouds into the sky.

2. After you have sampled your blue for your sky, if it is a bit dark or light, click the foreground color in the color picker and choose a blue from that same family that is better. Then click your background in the Color Picker and make that white.

If you wanted to put, say, a sunset in this photo, you could create a gradient for the sunset by taking similar color samples from another photo.

5. There are, of course, many other effects we could add here. For a convincing skywriting effect, write in a childlike printing with a soft 45-pixel airbrush on a new layer. Then on another layer, use the paintbrush preset "Fuzzy Cluster Loose." Some smudge to this layer as if the wind had messed up the letters a bit completes the realism.

3. Next, we can use a Linear Gradient (choose Linear Gradient in your gradient options bar) and drag it from top to bottom. Hold the SHIFT key to constrain it to perfectly vertical.

Resting in the Mushroom Patch

- Quick masks
- Transform
- Burn tool
- Levels
- Blur

3

In the last example, we took people out of a photograph. But what about adding people to a scene? In this example, we will take a person from one picture and add her to another.
Start by opening the two images we will be working with `janeerock.tif` and `morels.tif`

This will involve three steps :

- moving the one picture, the subject, onto another.

- masking out (or erasing) the background on the subject.

- doing whatever we need to blend the two images, in order to make it look like the woman actually belongs in this mushroom patch.

Putting the two images together

1. Make sure both the images are open in Photoshop and place them side-by-side on the desktop.

Using the Move tool, drag the woman on the rock over to the document with the mushrooms.

> If this doesn't work with your own images, then your documents are probably in different modes. To see if this is the case, go to **Image > Mode ...** for each and make sure that they are in RGB.

The Layers palette for our new document will look like this.

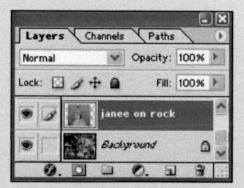

2. Go to **File > Save as...** and give the file a new name.

Masking out the background on the foreground image

Now we need to get rid of the ocean, before we can get a feeling for what else we have to do, such as sizing, coloring, shading, and so on.

Quick Mask mode is handy for this. What the Quick Mask does is to "protect" part of the image, much as a rubylith masking does in a "real" darkroom. It is often easier to color the rubylith on the subject, and then invert the mask. Then, if we convert the Quick Mask to a regular Layer mask, then we can edit our selection as we wish, affording us maximum flexibility.

1. To enter Quick Mask mode, type the letter Q.

2. Select a large hard round brush to start.

3. Color the subject, the part we are going to keep.

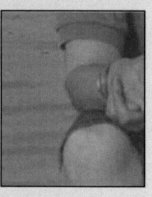

4. Next, we invert the mask, so that the background is covered in the rubylith. To do this, ALT/OPT-click the Exit Quick Mask button. This makes you exit Quick Mask mode and inverts the mask, which makes the woman the selection instead of the background. (You can, of course, paint the rubylith on the background to start with, but it is often easier to paint the subject.)

If you should happen to do this backwards, and find that you have made your subject disappear, then click up in the History palette to before you exited Quick Mask mode and then redo it the other way. I rarely get this right on the first time!

3

Making our sprite at home in the mushroom patch

A "fake" will often fall apart because of inconsistencies in the lighting, or because the shadows don't work. Perhaps something is not balanced right, or a component is the wrong size or color. In short, because it breaks the laws of physics!

In a certain light, an object is bound to cast a certain sort of shadow. No escaping that. So when we are doing a composition of this sort, we must account for it. The same light will hit objects from the same angle. Similarly, color hues, saturation, and brightness have to be appropriate.

For this example, there are a few things that we must do in order to make this work:
Resize the subject, our sprite.
- Adjust her surroundings.
- Touch up the mask.
- Fine-tune her position.
- Add shadows to the background.
- Add shadows to the sprite.
- Use adjustment layers as necessary to fix the levels and colors.
- Ease the crispness of the edges of the mask.
- Perfect the mask.

You can change the color of your Quick Mask, if the image you are working with is predominantly red, for example.

5. With your subject layer selected in the Layers palette, click on the Add Layer Mask button at the bottom of that palette now, and this should make your background disappear.

Changing the composition
As it is, she is far too large to sit comfortably here.

1. Press CTRL/⌘-T to bring up the Free Transform bounding box.

2. Hold down SHIFT as you drag your handles. This maintains the proportions.

3

Now that the sprite is resized, the rock she is sitting on doesn't look as good as we thought it might. Let's mask it out and leave her sitting on that leaf!

3. Because we have used a layer mask to take out the background, if we want to now take out that rock, we do that by painting over it in black on the mask.

 Note that if we decide later that we want this rock in the picture, we can bring it back by painting white back onto the mask!

4. Zoom in so that you get only the rock pixels and you do no damage to her feet, and paint out the rock. Also, at this point, it is good to zoom in close and paint out any stray ocean that may be hanging around the edges of our sprite.

No matter what tool you are using, you can zoom in without switching tools! Use CTRL/⌘-SPACE and click your image to zoom in. Use ALT/OPT-SPACE and click to zoom out!

Notice at this point that the shadows on the sprite are on her left side, but in this mushroom scene, she really needs to be shaded on her right side. So let's flip her over!

5. **Edit > Transform > Flip Horizontal** will fix this. This makes for a nicer composition too.

Changing the lighting and shading

Now that she is appropriately sized and flipped, let's concern ourselves with more of the physical reality of this picture.

First let's deal with the shadows. One way to get the shadows on the leaf is to burn that layer.

1. First, duplicate the background layer. Then on the topmost duplicate, using the Burn tool and a feathered brush, burn her a shadow. Going over it without picking up your brush will not deepen the burn – you have to lift your brush between strokes. Be sure to shade under her feet and legs, but not with as much intensity as where she sits. It is easy to overdo the burning.

Another way to handle this shadow is to paint one in. This is more easily controlled, since the subject is on its own layer.

2. To try this, delete the burned layer you just created, and make another layer above the background. Then use black with a wide feathered airbrush to paint in a shadow. Adjust the opacity by typing in a level, say 60, for 60%. (Typing just 6 works too, for this. Just type it. No boxes or windows.) Often, using a layer blending mode (like Color Burn or Multiply) with a shadow layer will ease it into the background even better. Experiment with the blending modes and see what they do.

4. To make this layer, first click on your Background layer to select it. Then click on the New Adjustment Layer button at the bottom of the Layers palette.

5. To lighten, go to **Image > Adjust > Levels**. Slide the light slider a bit left (220), the dark one a bit to the right (10), and the middle to the left until it looks right (1.36).

Oversaturation of colors often is a dead giveaway to a faked picture. Let's tone down the color of the figure a little, to make her blend in better with the forest floor.

6. Add a Hue/Saturation adjustment layer above our sprite's layer. To make the layer only affect the 'sprite' layer and not the background as well, hold down the ALT/OPT key whilst you hold your mouse right over the line below the adjustment layer. Then click your mouse on the special linked layers icon that appears. Desaturate the woman -30, to tone her down a little.

3. Our sprite also needs shading on her own layer on her right side, the side closer to the 'shrooms. This can be done with another layer and painting in a shadow, or you can do it with the Burn tool, directly on the layer. If you are burning right on the layer, it is always a good idea to duplicate your layer first.

7. A teensy levels adjustment (moving the midtone slider to 0.83) darkens the sprite just a bit, adding to the realism.

Our sprite among the mushrooms is a bit bright and a little too saturated. The background is a little too dark, too, for that matter. To lighten the background a bit, it works well to use an adjustment layer.

If you zoom in closely at this point, you will see that there are some very sharp edges around our subject. I especially find the lines around her hair to be too crisp.

One way to ease this crispness and make the image more natural is to add a little blur to the sprite's layer mask.

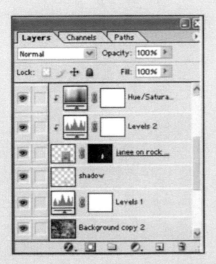

8. Click on the layer mask. Note that the paintbrush that is in the column next to the eye turns into a little layer mask icon to indicate that you are about to edit the mask, rather than the layer itself. Go to **Filter > Blur > Gaussian** Blur and add a blur of 1.1 pixels.

This just adds a bit of a blur, which is all you want. It doesn't blur the actual pixels of the image, but it actually adds back just a tiny bit of that background that she was in before we moved her. The effect is that of slight anti-aliasing, rather than actual blurring.

After doing this, the one final step you might need to perform is to perfect the mask, if part of your image needs to be made more crisp.

For this image, her left shoulder needs reworking in this way, because the sunshine on it requires a clear demarcation.

9. Click the layer mask, and go back over the edge of the mask with your paintbrush, to add that bit of sharpness.

3

Wren in pink

- Levels
- Clone Stamp tool
- Sample painting
- Liquify filter
- Masking

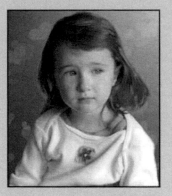

3

This is one of those rare moments captured, when we wish that the backdrop was pretty much anything else! First of all, as a photographer, you know that you would have been much better off setting up a good shot beforehand. Having failed that, however, is there any hope for this photo?

Assuming that we want to make this candid shot into a portrait, we must analyze this to see what we can do, and how best to undertake it. The most important task is changing the background. It would be desirable, too, to get rid of the cup, and to remove Aunt Becky's hands from in front of Wren's arms. Some Levels work is in order, as well, to bring out the light in the little girl's face.

Open `wren.psd` from the chapter folder.

1. We'll start with a Levels adjustment. You get maximum flexibility with adjustments like this if you do it through an adjustment layer. Moving the middle slider a little to the left takes out just enough of the darkness.

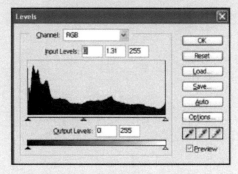

Next we tackle the tough stuff, cloning out the hand and the cup. When you are "taking out" something from a picture like this, you don't actually remove anything. You are really converting the pixels that are there to what you would like them to be. One way that this is frequently done is through cloning.

To "take out" Aunt Becky's hands, for example, we are actually putting Wren's shirt in where the hand pixels are. Cloning enables us to sample nearby pixels or groups of pixels and copy them into the new location. Often there is some artistry involved in this, because we are really remaking what should be there.

2. Make a new layer by clicking the New Layer icon at the bottom of the Layers palette.

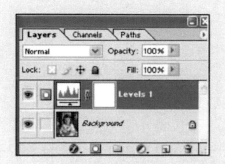

3. Select the Clone Stamp tool. Check Use All Layers and Aligned in the options bar. Hold down the ALT/OPT key, click your mouse to sample, and then use your Clone Stamp tool to copy the pixels to the new location. Since you are doing this on a new layer, if you mess up, you can always erase the offending part and do it over.

In a complex arrangement such as this shirt, with all of its wrinkling, it is difficult to get a good cloning result, as you can see here.

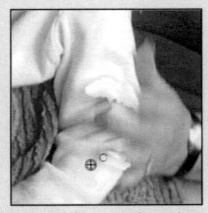

If it becomes too time-consuming to clone and try to make it look good, it is often more expedient to sample paint the pixels in.

4. To do sample painting, choose your Brush tool and a small feathered brush. You can change the size of your brush easily with the] and [on your keyboard. Holding down the ALT/OPT key and clicking on a place on your canvas serves to sample that color, making it the foreground color. This enables you to paint with that color. By sampling often, and using a small brush, you can come very close to replicating the folds of this shirt.

5. We remove the cup in much the same way, by adding skirt and shirt pixels, through cloning.

Though the pattern of her skirt is a regular one, it is not quite as regular as the effect we get from this cloning.

6. To make the skirt's pattern a little less regular, try using **Filter > Liquify**. The swirl brushes used sparingly will produce a nice, slightly irregular effect.

The idea is to make it so that, while imperfection does not attract our attention, perfection does not catch our eye either, so that we maintain the illusion of realism.

3

3

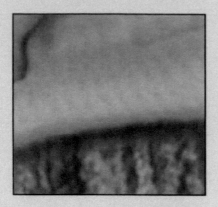

In cloning, one problem that we can encounter is an effect called "patterning", which we saw earlier in our lighthouse example. This occurs when you don't resample, but keep on painting with new strokes.

7. You can fix the patterning effect by creating a new layer over the top of our image, and sample painting over it, in tones of white, mottling it with some gray, to match the texture of the rest of the shirt.

8. To make the edges look more natural, where her skirt and shirt join, sample paint on yet another layer this darker ridge on the shirt, and the deeper pink ridge on the top of the skirt.

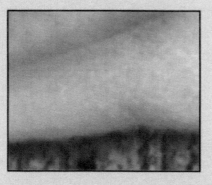

If this is too intense an effect, you can lower the opacity of this layer. It could also be effective to employ a different layer blending mode, such as multiply, darken, or overlay, for this painted corrections layer.

Get into the habit of labeling your layers as you add them. Though it seems unnecessary in the beginning, (how could I possibly forget what this layer is for?) as the number of your layers increases, it becomes rapidly very handy to have them labeled. To label a layer easily in Photoshop 7, double-click the layer name in the Layers palette and type it in.

Removing the background

Now to whisk Wren out of her Aunt Becky's arms, so that we can put her into a different, more portrait-like background. There are many ways to remove the background of a picture.

Protecting the work

Before we work further on the background, we have a little more "backup" work to do. Because your mask needs to include all of the painted and cloned layers, it is easiest to do this if you first flatten these with the main picture. Flattening, however, makes me nervous, so I like to duplicate all the involved layers first, flattening only one set of them.

If you have several layers to duplicate, here is one way to make this job more tidy:

- *Link all of the layers you are going to ulti mately flatten.*
- *Click the little arrow to the top right on the Layers palette and choose "New Set from Linked."*
- *Right-click the new Layer Set in the Layers palette and choose "Duplicate Layer Set."*
- *Turn off the eye for one of these duplicate sets.*
- *Click that arrow to the top right in the Layers palette again and this time click on Merge Layer Set. This merged layer set is the layer on which you will take away the background.*

Removing the background

Now to take out the background. First we need to make a loose selection around the subject.

1. Choose the Lasso tool and use it to trace a loose border around the subject. Be sure to incorporate all of her, including wispy hairs.

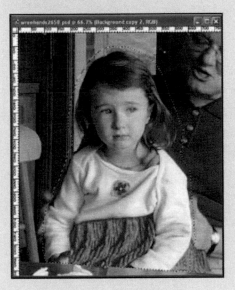

2. Convert the selection into a layer mask. Click the subject's layer in the Layers palette and then click the Add Layer Mask button at the bottom of that palette.

It is often easier to get a clean masking if you are working against some background other than the default checkerboard. In fact, switching background colors as you work can be very helpful, to make sure that you are cleaning out the right colors of pixels. If you are doing your masking against white, your job will often look MUCH different against black.

3. Click the New Layer icon at the bottom of the Layers palette and then drag this new layer below the subject's layer. Choose a medium gray, to begin with, and ALT/OPT-BACKSPACE to fill your layer.

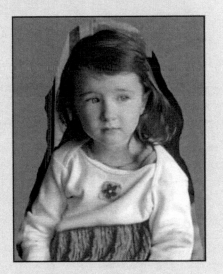

4. Highlight your subject layer, and then click on its layer mask. Notice that little layer mask icon again.

5. Now take a round brush, a relatively wide one at first, with spacing set to just 1%. Using black, color in around the outside of your image. Zoom in when it is necessary. If you color too much of the edge, you can undo this with the same brush and white. Layer masks are very versatile indeed, affording you the maximum in control.

3

3

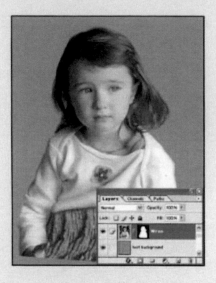

The final step is to change the background to one that looks like a portrait backdrop.

6. Either put your desired background layer under her, or drag her over to a new background document. (Her layer mask will come with her.)

When you do this, you will be likely to find areas around the edge that are too light or too dark. Generally, a feathered brush at this point will be good for these touchups. Feathering leaves the mask pixels gray and this means that the pixels it controls will be partially visible!

So here is Wren against a number of different backgrounds. Personally I think that the slightly darker backdrop works better, as it is more in keeping with the lighting of the original photo, but this balance is something you can play with, as we saw in earlier examples.

Cleaning up the countryside

- Cloning
- Sample painting
- Lasso tool
- Gradients
- Gaussian blur
- Magic Wand tool

3

In this example, we will take a tranquil pastoral scene and remove the blights upon its beauty. Open `fencerow.psd`.

In particular, we will remove the sign, and the overhead wires and poles, plus that bit of trash by the roadside. One little composition error is bothersome, as well – the second fencepost spearing the hay bale. We will correct that. This image presents some challenges because so much of it is gradients of color, but let's dive in and see how we can tackle this.

1. Start by protecting your image. Go to **File > Save As..** and name it something else. Save it in .psd format so that for subsequent saves, your layers will be intact. Next, drag your layer to the New Layer icon to duplicate it, just in case you accidentally start cloning on the main image instead of on your cloning layer. Make a new layer and name it "cloning" or something equally clever.

2. Choose your Clone Stamp tool from your toolbox. Check both Aligned and Use All Layers. Now zoom in till you are not squinting to see the wires and poles and then you are ready to go!

3. Sample often, and use a fairly small brush. Working on this image at 1600 x 1200, a 10-pixel brush is a

reasonable choice to begin with.

You want the area behind the sign to look realistic and natural, of course, so take care to keep the blades of grass looking right. Using vertical strokes helps with this.

3

As you work on this, it can start looking surreal! It really feels like you are doing the impossible. Picking up trash was never this easy before!

When we get to the trees with the poles in front of them, this presents a problem. That is because there are not many pixels nearby for us to sample. In this situation, all too often, it is easy to develop patterning, where the sampled pixels are repeated over and over yielding a disturbingly unnatural result.

4. To repair the patterning that developed here, a bit of sample painting works nicely. If you are thinking that you are a photographer and not a painter, I urge you to try this, nonetheless.

- Do this on a new clean layer, so it will be easy to fix if you happen to mess it up.
- Zoom in very closely so that it no longer looks like trees and you see that it is just pixels to paint!
- Use a very small brush (I prefer a hard brush for this) and sample often, just leaving little bits of paint.

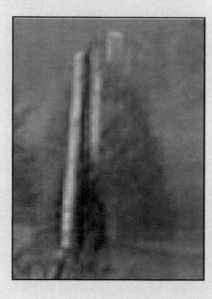

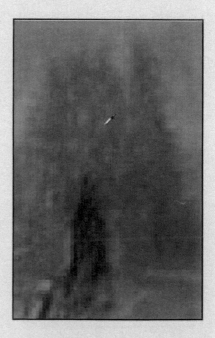

3

Use similar techniques to get rid of the trash and the telephone poles.

Next, let's do that little composition correction for the post. Shortening it will work. Moving the haybale would work much the same way, though. Amazing what we can do with Photoshop! To shorten the fencepost, here is one way to proceed:

8. CTRL/⌘-SPACE-click to zoom in and, using a very small brush, clone in the grass and the front of the haybale, using surrounding areas to sample.

5. Draw a selection around the fencepost top using the Lasso tool.

Another difficulty is this sky. It is difficult to get a gradient sky like this to look even from just cloning. There are numerous ways to fix this, one of which would be to build a new sky. However, this sky speaks of a particular early-morning moment, so let's keep it. Here is another way to fix this.

6. Put a copy of the selection onto a new layer by pressing CTRL/⌘-J.

7. Drag the fencepost top down till it clears the haybale.

9. Make an elliptical selection that well covers the problem area.

10. Click the foreground color in your color picker and sample the lightest color within the ellipse.

11. Click the background color in the color picker and sample the darkest color within the ellipse.

12. Make a new layer.

13. Choose the Gradient tool, foreground to background, and sweep a Linear Gradient across your ellipse.

Now it *really* looks fake! We better fix it.

14. CTRL/⌘-D to deselect.

15. Go to **Filter > Blur > Gaussian Blur** and choose an extreme value of blur. For this example, 60 pixels worked well.

Now the sky looks good, but it spills over onto the hills. We don't want quite that much haze! Here's how to fix it:

16. Type W to choose the Magic Wand tool. Check Use All Layers, have Contiguous on, and use a fairly high tolerance, say, 50 pixels.

17. Tap your wand on the lower part of the sky, as shown here:

18. Go to **Select > Feather** and enter 2 pixels. This will soften your edge a bit. (Don't forget to change this setting back when you are finished with this, or you will wonder later why your selections are fuzzy!)

19. Make sure that you have the 'ellipse' layer, and then go to **Select > Inverse** and hit the DELETE key.

And here is our pristine pastoral scene!

3

3

Conference room switch

- Move tool
- Levels
- Masking
- Sample painting
- Sharpen filter

You know how it goes, when you are trying for a good group shot. There is generally someone with a silly expression, or their eyes closed. Perhaps someone is even missing altogether and needs to be put into the picture. Or perhaps one employee has been replaced by another and a head-switch is in order. In this example, we'll address all of these concerns!

It is handy to have two shots from the same sitting with which to work. This simplifies lighting concerns, sizing issues, and position, to some extent. I will call the two images from which we will work, "source" and "target," with our target image the one which will ultimately be our finished project.

Begin by having a good look at your target image and determine what problems you wish to solve. In this image, once we fix the coloring and levels, we need to open Susan's eyes and fix Kelly's surprised expression. Finally, we will add Carolyn, who was not present for this photo opportunity.

Protect your work! Save as... and come up with a different name for your work-in-progress. Save it as a psd file, so that you can keep your layers intact. Then, before you do any changes to the actual image itself, duplicate its layer. Use adjustment layers where possible, and do corrections on new layers where possible. If your layers become unwieldy, you can group them into layer sets. If you feel you must flatten or merge layers, consider Save as.. and give your file yet another name. This way you will have a version that still has all your layers intact!

Fixing levels and coloring is best left until after your body-switches, if your source document has the same coloring as the target. In this example, however, there are two different lighting arrangements, and the coloring is not a factor. We can first adjust this on our target document, and do necessary adjustments to any add-ins as we need to.

1. Click the "Create New Fill or Adjustment Layer" button at the bottom of the Layers palette and choose Levels. Just a bit of movement on the middle slider is all that's required here.

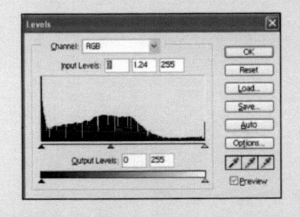

2. Since the lighting is fluorescent, let's add some blue, using **Image > Adjustments > Variations**. This really improves the color balance.

We are fortunate in that we have a source image that has many very usable spare parts, including a fine head for Susan, and one for Kelly.

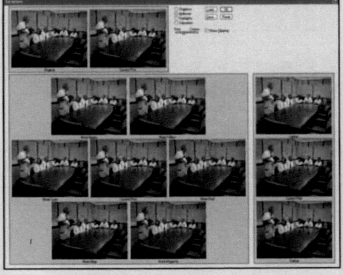

We will take Carolyn from another picture where she is sitting just how she should be in our target image.

3

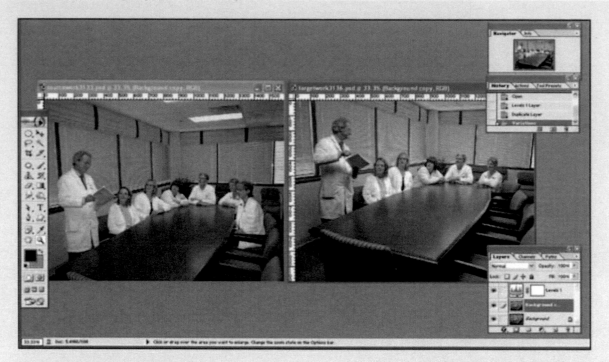

Changing Kelly's head

1. Open the source document and set it alongside the target, on the desktop. Zoom in on Kelly in the source document and select her head, using your favorite selection method. The Lasso tool is one good choice. Because of the evenness of her skin-tones and the fact that there is no noticeable demarcation between her chin color and her neck color, selecting down into her clothing works well here.

2. While you have the selection ants marching, zoom back out till you can see both images on your desktop. Choose the Move tool and put it inside the selection and notice that it turns into scissors. This indicates that we can now cut Kelly's head out of there. Drag her new head into your target image.

When using your own images, if the selection won't permit itself to be dragged, be sure that both images are in RGB mode.

Here's how to solve this: Click the Create New Adjustment Layer icon at the bottom of the Layers palette. Choose what you want to adjust: levels, in this case. Without changing anything, click OK in that box. Position your pointer on the line between the adjustment layer and the layer just below it. Hold down the ALT/OPT key and click when you see the little Clipping Group icon. Now you can make your adjustments to just that one layer by double-clicking the levels thumbnail (not the mask) in the Layers palette.

3

Before we move it into place, we need to ascertain what changes we have to make, in order to make this convincing. Pay attention to the sizes; they need to match. Reducing the opacity of your new head can help in getting the size right. Adjust opacity at the top of the Layers palette. Also, there may be times when you have to rotate your transplanted head a bit. In Kelly's case, the lightness of the replacement head is the most important correction to make.

3. Compare the coloring of the new head with her old one. For Kelly, just a touch of Levels adjustment, as shown below, brought her skin tone in line with her coloring in the target photo.

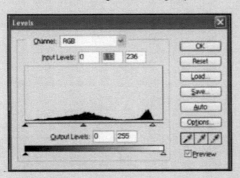

Other photos may need other adjustments, such as Hue/Saturation.

The problem with adjusting levels to just her head is that either you do the adjustment to the actual head layer, or you ADD an adjustment layer, which is safer and more versatile. But if you add an adjustment layer, it will adjust everything that is below it - not a good thing.

4. Use the Move tool to move Kelly's new head over to where it needs to be. Now it becomes apparent that we have a few minor adjustments to make.

Her jacket didn't line up quite the same in both of the shots, so we have to fix that. Also, there are some parts of her hair where the cutoff is too abrupt.

5. Here's one way to fix this. With Kelly's head layer selected in the Layers palette, click the Add Layer Mask icon at the bottom of the Layers palette. Then choose a small, feathered brush and paint away, in black, the parts that you do not like, including the edges of her hair and that neckline.

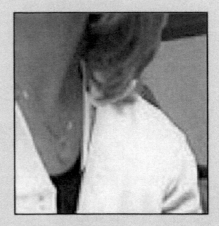

3

6. Her eyeglasses on the replacement photo have that bit of glare in them, so we can (on a new layer!) sample-paint over that. ALT/OPT-click with your small brush to grab a sample of the color you want. (Sampling will sample whatever is visible, regardless of what layer you are working on), then paint on your new layer. Her left lens looks a bit darker than the right one. Fix this by selecting her right lens (on our left) with the Lasso and then applying the Burn tool with a wide feathered brush at 50%.

Replacing Susan's head
We will do Susan's head in much the same way.

1. Bring up your source document again.

2. Press CTRL/⌘-D to drop any current selections.

3. Now zoom in on Susan and trace around her with the Lasso tool. Again, as long as you get all of her, you don't have to worry about getting a very precise selection.

Notice that we are trimming down into her clothing. This is because of the different tilt of her head from the source photo to the target. We could rotate the replacement head to match the tilt of the old one, but this is rather a nice tilt, don't you think?

4. Drag Susan's head over to the other image. Again, reduce the opacity if it makes it easier.

5. Now, adjust Levels to lighten her a bit. Again, her coloring seems a good match at this point. The size is perfect.

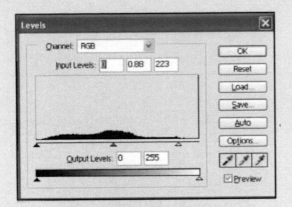

After you fix Susan's neckline by masking away that collar (which mysteriously turned.. blue?), you end up with this frightful neck-effect. The following method works because our image is small, so there is not much detail present.

6. Using the Move tool, drag Susan's head into place in the Target image.

7. After you get Susan's head where you want it, add a layer mask to her layer and, on this mask, run around the fringy outsides with a feathered brush, as you did with Kelly. You can even brush it over her hair to bring out the blonder highlights that were more apparent in the original lighting. Mask away the collar as well.

8. Use a white paintbrush to "erase" the corrections you made on the layer mask around the bottom of Susan's neck.

9. Click on the layer itself in the Layers palette, so that you can work on that, and then take the Smudge tool and smudge using downward strokes, dragging the top image's neck colors down so that it just hides the edge of her collar. Now click back to your mask. Using your black brush, color your

mask along the collar line so that the extra neck disappears below the collar.

The result: Susan looks as if she had not been changed at all!

Susan's neck is still too thick, too evenly-toned, and her hair still carries some remnants of the old hair on the right side of the picture.

10. To fix these, click the main image layer and then click the Add New Layer icon to make another layer. Now clone Kelly's coat to cover the old Susan's hair tufts. Check Use All Layers, or it will try to clone nothing (from the new layer) onto nothing.

11. To shape Susan's neck better and give it a little color differentiation, first add another layer above the levels layer for her new head. Onto this layer, clone a bit of her hair from the left side of the photo onto her neck, leaving it wispy and natural. Then, with a small soft airbrush, sample-paint the left side (our left) of her neck, grabbing three or four color samples from her forehead and cheeks. Make your strokes subtle and do use a few different shades.

Adding Carolyn to the picture

Now that Kelly and Susan are happily modeling their new heads, we need to get Carolyn into the picture! Selecting part of her chair and running the lasso along the dark delineations make this a bit easier. Of course, having the photo taken at the same sitting and at the same angle helps immeasurably, as well.

1. Select her from the second source image and drag her into this picture as we did with Kelly and Susan. A tweak of the Levels adjustment, and one in the Color Balance, as shown, brings her color in line with the rest of the group.

2. On a new layer, sample the arm color from another chair and then stroke it in. The little highlight takes away the flatness.

3

3. Running Carolyn's layer through **Filter > Sharpen > Unsharp Mask** with a setting of 50% and 2 pixels sharpens her just enough to complete this picture.

Then we have the problem of getting the rest of the picture to fit in. Because we selected so loosely, and because of the similarity of the two photos, the target and the source, there isn't much work to do. The chair needs some painting correction.

77

Keep in mind that these methods, while they may work well with these examples, will certainly not take care of every situation. Practice and experience in doing this kind of work will help you in deciding how to approach a problem image.

3

3

Chapter 4
Restoring and Repairing Photos

Photographers and other image professionals are often interested in making new images look old, or in making old images look new. In restoration work, our aim is different. We are not trying to make an old or damaged photo look new, but to make it look as it did, way back when Grandmother first saw it as she sat in Great Grandpa's arms. So we are making the photo look new, but new by the standards of a different era – almost as if we were transporting ourselves, the viewers, back in time!

Therefore, details of work like coloring a photo or changing color tones, such as sepia-toning a photo that was not sepia to start with, will be left for other chapters. These procedures, while they can certainly add to the appeal of a photo, are enhancements, but are not, strictly speaking, restorative.

However, there are color changes that are restorative. In this chapter, we will be working with several monochromatic photos, which have, through the passage of the years, accumulated off-tones, such as green or yellow, or have seen their color fade considerably. We will be attempting here to restore the color to its original condition.

Now, of course we cannot know exactly what the photo was like 100 years ago. Photo restoration does incorporate some artistic license, and a certain amount of guesswork, which we'll be making use of here, as you will in your own restorative work later.

Photo restoration and repair is a complex art. It would not be difficult to fill a thick book (or two) with details on various types of photo restorations, and solving many of the problems inherent in such work. However, even in the most complete book, you will not find all the answers. For every photo you restore or repair, you will encounter unique problems and situations. Time and practice will enable you to approach this work with the confidence gained from experience.

Please do not expect this work to go fast and smoothly all the time. Although restoration work is very rewarding, both emotionally and, if we are good enough, financially, it is also time-consuming and, at times, tedious. Patience will often be rewarded with a beautiful picture. Haste will usually be punished by a poor result.

The restoration process

In this chapter, we will look at several techniques that are used to restore and repair photos. Your own photos are likely to present very different challenges. Therefore, I suggest that you first practice a bit by working with the images we provide along with this book for this purpose. After you have gained some confidence with these methods by working on our examples, you will be more able to evaluate and solve your problems with your own.

We're going to explore Photoshop techniques to digitally accomplish the following:

- Remove dust, scratches, and mold or mildew.
- Repair torn, cracked, or creased photos.
- Restore faded photos, and photos where they are faded unevenly.

Before we jump right in to the examples, let's have a look at the processes we will go through in a little more detail.

Evaluating a problem photo

You should always begin by taking a long hard look at what you want to achieve, and how you intend to go about it. This may seem obvious, but it is tempting, at times, to jump into a photo restoration with both feet, without any clear goals. When we do this, sometimes we end up doing work that turns out to be unnecessary, or having to redo part of the work just because we did not plan well. Once I worked for over an hour to clone out scratches in a background, and, upon looking more closely, I decided to replace that background entirely.

In a similar vein, it is important to evaluate your work from time to time as it is in progress. Don't get obsessed with making perfectly smoothed areas in a part of the picture if that level of smoothness doesn't match the rest of what you have done.

If you are evaluating a job to do for a prospective client, it is critical that you and your client have a clear understanding of what you are to do with your restoration. There are different amounts of work that you could do, depending upon the result that the client wants. If you estimate only for removing dust and a few scratches and correcting the tonal contrast, then make sure that your client understands that is just what you will do. Make sure that there is clear understanding that this will not cover, for example, replacing part of the picture that was torn away. Although sometimes we can perform what looks like a miracle, using Photoshop, it is not actually

magic, and if you are working for someone else, you need to make clear the limitations of the process.

Protecting your work

I am assuming you backup your work each night (stern look). I was once told that it isn't a question of **if** your hard drive is going to crash, it is a question of **when**. Back up to a second hard drive, to a Zip or a CD at regular intervals. If you are staying busy, back up nightly. Keeping a remote copy of important files is good, especially if you depend upon your computer for your livelihood.

Second, **duplicate your image layer**. Take a moment when you first begin work to drag that Background layer, your photo layer, to the Add New Layer icon in the Layers palette to duplicate it. Turn off the eye. You should work on a duplicate layer of your photo, or on a layer above it, but not on the original photo. Of course, you will have saved your original in another document, but this is an easy way to have a little mini-backup right on your desktop.

Color and tonal corrections

One of the first things you will want to do is to correct the tones and colors in your photo. I always prefer to use **Adjustment Layers** for these operations. Adjustment layers are like special overlays, not changing the actual pixels of our photo underneath. We can even go in and fix the adjustment later if we need to.

We will be working extensively with adjustment layers for color corrections in this chapter. We will work with all of the great features that make adjustment layers so useful. We'll be hiding part of an adjustment layer, using its mask, so that it only affects the parts of the image that need it, and applying a blending mode to the adjustment layers to intensify certain effects.

We will be using Curves and Levels for tonal correction and improving contrast.

Removing dust and small imperfections

Many old photos have little spots on them, whether from dust or from being worn. We will work with the Healing Brush tool, Clone Stamp tool, blur-painting, layer blending modes, and sample painting to fix these.

4

Prevention is better than any of the cures, of course, but it is quite possible, using Photoshop, to clean up even the grossest fungus. We will use the Clone Stamp tool and a bit of sample painting to clean up these problems.

Fixing tears and replacing missing parts

It is really surprising just how much abuse a photo can take, but yet its owner still clings to the hope that it can be fixed. I am of the belief that any photo can be recreated, given enough time and, if necessary, spare parts – that is, other photos of the same subjects with which to work. This can be really difficult, time-consuming and, when it is done well, nothing short of amazing. We will be fixing a torn picture in our example, A Good Boy. There are only a few minor areas of this photo that need to be replaced and we will be able to accomplish this with the other tools.

4

Young patriot

- Using Levels and Curves to make tonal adjustments
- Blur-painting
- Healing Brush tool
- Clone Stamp tool
- Patch tool
- Sample painting
- Dodge tool
- Burn tool

4

This photo is a scan at 600ppi of a photo that is little bigger than a postage stamp! Let's start restoring it to its former beauty.

Evaluation of the photo

Let's begin our task by looking at what we need to fix here:

- Adjusting the tone and contrast.
- Removing dust / mold on the top of the photo.
- Getting rid of the mold at the bottom of photo.
- Removing dust or mold on her face and blouse.
- Repairing scratches and "missing" areas of white in her hair.
- Fixing the flag - a missing area and the faded stripe.
- Fixing and enhancing her eyes.
- Removing the faint darkish horizontal lines across her mouth.
- Sorting out the darkness across the bottom of the photo.

1. First, drag your layer to the New Layer icon at the bottom of the Layers Palette to duplicate the layer, and turn off the eye on the lower layer. This leaves us with a handy backup of the original within our working file.

2. Using your top layer as your working layer, desaturate this photo. Since it is monochrome, any other colors that may have been scanned in will just serve as noise and will get in the way of our work. There are at least two ways to desaturate:

- You can use an adjustment layer by clicking the Add Adjustment Layer icon at the bottom of the Layers palette and choosing Hue/Saturation.
- You can use the menu bar at the top, by going to **Image > Adjustment > Desaturate**.

I used the second method, as we know we have a backup since we duplicated the 'background' layer to begin with.

3. Duplicate the desaturated layer and rename it 'working copy'.

Next we need to make the decision as to how we are going to deal with the task of adjusting the tones and contrast.

Levels or Curves?

Levels are easier to deal with because you only have the three components with which to work: Highlights, Shadows, and Midtones. You can access Levels by clicking the Add Adjustment Layer icon at the bottom of the Layers palette (or going to **Layer > New Adjustment Layer > Levels...**).

There are several different approaches you can use for working with Levels. One way is to use the sliders:

4. Pull the white slider over toward the left until it is right under where the histogram begins, that is, where the pixels shades begin in the photo. This will define the pixels above and to the right of the slider as pure **white** and will lighten the rest of the image to conform to that.

5. Pull the black slider over toward the right until it is right under where the histogram begins on the left side. Similarly, this will define the pixels represented in the histogram above and to the left of the slider to be **black**.

6. Pull the Midtone (central) slider to the left or the right until the image looks right to you.

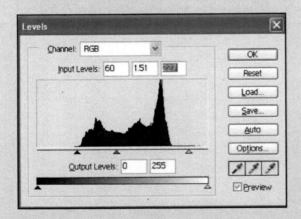

You can also use the eyedroppers to adjust levels.

To do this, choose the white (rightmost) eyedropper and touch it to a point on the photo that you wish to be pure white (called the **Whitepoint**). It will make that point and anything lighter than that pure white. You can do the same with the black one. If you are not careful, this is an easy way to lose detail,.

Curves

Curves are a more versatile, albeit more complex, way to adjust your tones and contrast. Although it is possible to learn what curves will do to your image by experimentation, it will speed up your learning if you take a few minutes to understand how they work.

The curve is a graphical representation of how you change each tone of your image. Go to **Layer > New Adjustment Layer > Curves**. When you first open your Curves adjustment layer, the "curve" is a straight segment, stretching from the dark-dark corner up to the light-light corner. Before you have adjusted the curve, the light **input values**, that is, the tones that are now in your photo, are represented by the right side of the horizontal axis. The dark input values are represented by the left side of the horizontal axis.

So what about the vertical axis? This is your **output** scale, that is, what tonal values you are creating for your image. Before you adjust the curve, the values for the horizontal axis and the vertical axis are identical. Your inputs are equal to your outputs for every tonal value from dark to light.

In the picture below, the purple line marks one point that is fairly dark, and the green represents a point that is fairly light.

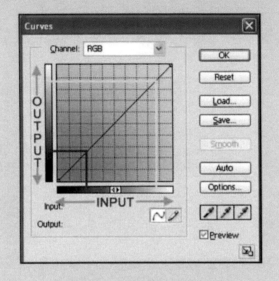

As we move the purple point up vertically, the tonal value for this color gets lighter. At the same time all of the other tonal values in the photo will become lighter, in a precise relationship. Notice how the whole curve bends just from moving one point? This is how Photoshop protects the photo from drastic tonal swings.

When you move a point on your curve, all of the points that have the same tonal value as those at the purple line become lighter.

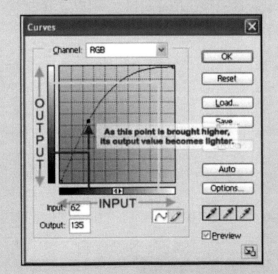

Curves are pretty touchy. Your picture can get very different very fast, if you greatly change a point's location, or if you move lots of points around. To see what I mean, make a curve that looks like an "M." What you are telling it to do when you make the curve into, say, an M, is to make the pixels that are now either very dark or very light, very dark. The pixels that are midway between black and gray (in brightness) or between white and gray will be made white. The pixels that are now middle-of-the-road gray become black.

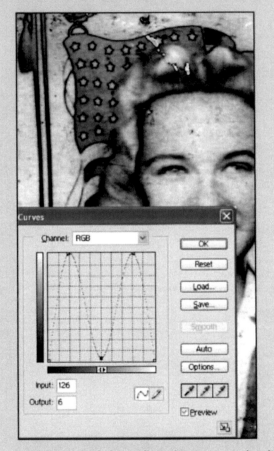

7. Press Reset, and then adjust the curve so that it looks more like this "standard" S-curve.

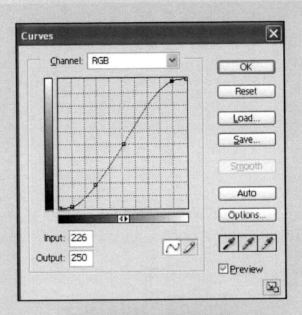

The lighter midtones are made a bit lighter and the darker ones are made a bit darker. This has the effect of increasing the contrast, but in a very controlled way (especially in comparison to Levels).

8. As we have used adjustment layers for adjusting the tone and contrast, we are afforded maximum flexibility. Click the eyes next to the adjustment layers on and off, to see the difference. Whether to use Levels or Curves is up to you. I liked the effect produced by Curves, so I trashed the Levels adjustment layer.

There are a lot of areas in the image where we need to sort out blemishes on the surface of the photo. What tool you use will depend on the type of damage, and the textures that you are trying to recreate.

Blur painting

Before the Healing Brush tool came along, blur painting was one of the more popular approaches to fixing minor damage. It was most useful when we had minor blemishes on a smooth and homogeneous background. There are times when it is not appropriate to use blur painting. It is not good for working with detailed areas or complex textures. It won't work well when contrasting colors abut each other, either. We will explore these limitations in this section.

Although the Healing Brush tool largely replaces blur painting, there are some lessons to be learned from working through the process. The best way to see what the technique does is to actually do some. So pick up your brush! Here's how it's done:

1. Duplicate your 'background copy' layer again, and rename it 'blurred'.

2. You should have an untouched background layer with the eye turned off, the copy of the background layer above that, your new one which is the "blurred" layer, and a fourth, your 'working copy' layer, above that. Finally, the Curves adjustment layer should be uppermost, at the top of the Layers palette.

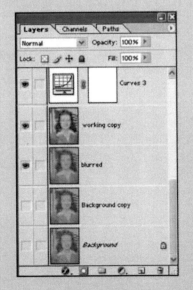

4

2. Turn the eye off on your 'working copy' layer.

3. Select the 'blurred' layer in the Layers palette, and go to **Filter > Blur > Gaussian Blur**. The amount of blur will vary depending upon the size of your image, but you should blur it until the features are not recognizable, but there is still some delineation between them. For this image, I used a radius of 9.2.

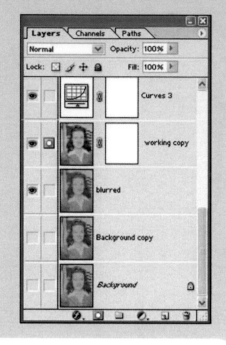

Gaussian Blur

OK

Reset

☑ Preview

100%

Radius: 9.2 pixels

4. Now make the 'working copy' layer visible again, and click it in the Layers palette to select it.

5. Click the Add Layer Mask button at the bottom of the Layers palette. Click on the mask so that you are painting on it and not your working layer itself. (The little brush beside the eye in the Layers palette turns into a layer mask icon to indicate you are painting on the mask.)

Painting black on a layer mask is like cutting a hole in your layer, which permits the layer below to show. Layer masks are very versatile and useful for many tasks. They are my favorite way to blend two pictures together, for example. Using a mask to cut an object from its background leaves us with the freedom to correct the selection, to add to or subtract from it. By contrast, using an eraser is permanent. Once those pixels are erased, you are not going to bring them back, unless, of course, you have duplicated your layer. Even then, though, it is troublesome to fix mistakes. If you have not yet worked with these little jewels of Photoshop, I encourage you use this as your nudge!

Now this is the part that seems a bit like magic.

6. Choose a 2 or 3-pixel soft brush and gently paint away some of the small isolated dust specks.

7. What you are actually doing here is painting on the layer mask – in effect, cutting a little (reparable) hole in the working layer, which lets the blurred area peek through. If you are working with a tablet and stylus, using a light touch here will yield better results.

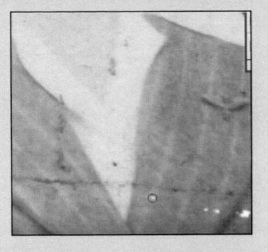

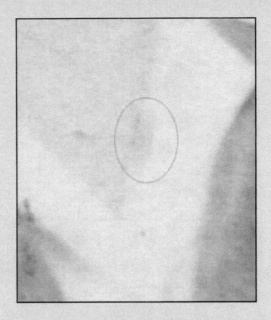

4

Well if this is as good as it seems, we should be able to paint away all of life's problems with blur, right?

Not quite. There are a couple of problems with using the blur-painting technique. One is that you lose texture, especially if the spot you are removing is not very small.

In this picture, you see how the spot in the blue circle, when painted out, became just another problem, a textureless area.

If you find that you want to correct something that you have done in blur painting, type X. This switches your foreground and background colors, so you can paint in white, erasing what you had done. If you want to toss the whole mask, you can do that by clicking on it in the Layers palette and dragging it to the trash can.

Healing Brush tool

With the advent of Photoshop 7, comes the Healing Brush tool! This little jewel takes what is there and what you tell it you want there and, almost magically, "heals" the area. You have to try this to believe it, really. A few things that you need to know first though:

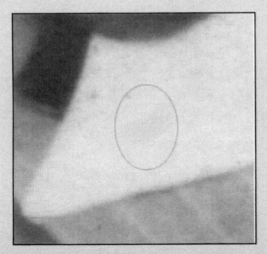

Another problem with this technique is shown in this picture. If you try to fix an area that is not isolated, that is, it is on one color that is close to where another color joins, the blurred layer will include some of the other color, leaving blended muddy colors, a most undesirable result.

1. To use the Healing Brush tool, you have to work on the actual working layer, so duplicate this (yes, again!) before you do this work.

2. ALT/OPT-click an area of your image that you want to use as the source to heal the damaged part. Your pointer will become a cross-hair while the ALT/OPT key is held down.

3. If you are working on an area that is close to another area of contrasting colors, make a selection around the part you want to heal first. Isolating your target area keeps the surrounding pixels from interfering with your pixel "color-averaging." When you try to heal in two areas that are contrasting, you can get a "bleed" effect from one area into the other.

4

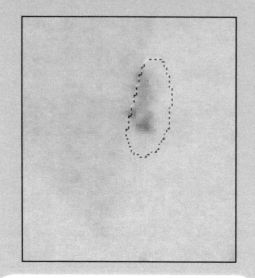

1. To use the Clone Stamp tool, first make a new layer above your working layer, but beneath the adjustment layer. Rename this 'cloning corrections'.

2. Then check Use All Layers in the Clone Stamp tool options bar. This will enable you to clone from what you see on any other layers onto your fresh new layer. If you should mess up an area and wish to redo it, you can simply erase from your new layer. If, however, you were cloning onto your main working layer, you do not have that freedom. By default, the History palette is only set to record the last 20 steps, and even if you have set it higher than this, it is amazing how fast you can gather steps when you are cloning!

3. ALT/OPT-click the source area and then paint over your problem area.

If you are suddenly unable to get your tools to work and you have checked everything, but still nothing is working, be sure that you don't have a tiny selection going on your canvas. CTRL/⌘-D will deselect, if this is the case. Also, be sure to check that you are working on a visible layer, that the opacity of the layer and its blending mode are what you expect, that the blending mode of your tool is ok, that the opacity of your tool isn't zero, and that you are painting on the actual layer, and not on the layer mask, if that is what you intend to do. If you are intending to paint on your mask, be sure that, if the background is white, you are not trying to paint with white. Does it sound as if I learned all of this the hard way?

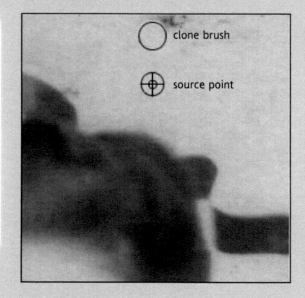

clone brush

source point

Clone Stamp tool

The Clone Stamp tool remains, probably, the best way to handle large-scale image fixes, the big moldy areas of a photo we are restoring for example. The Clone Stamp tool permits you to sample an area and then paint with that sample, the width and shape of your brush, into a different area. If you have Aligned checked, the sampling will follow along at the same distance and angle as you paint. If you don't use this checkbox, your cloning will keep taking from the same area, starting in the same place every time you lift your brush.

4. Sample often, and use a small brush, especially for fine areas. I actually prefer to use a hard brush for this, as it affords me more control over individual pixels, especially in areas where there is marked contrast between light and dark values. If you want softness, a soft brush might serve well. If your changes are subtle, you can also do well using a brush with less than 100% opacity. To make your opacity, say, 60%, type the number 6. You can also change it using the setting in the options bar.

5. If you need to repair a large area and have only a small source area from which to sample, you have to be vigilant about the possibility of patterning as you clone. Patterning is the annoying repetition of the same arrangement of pixels. You can often avoid it by frequently sampling from different areas of your photo, and from using a small brush. If your source area is too small to clone without getting this patterning effect, you may wish to repair the area using sample painting, a technique I describe below.

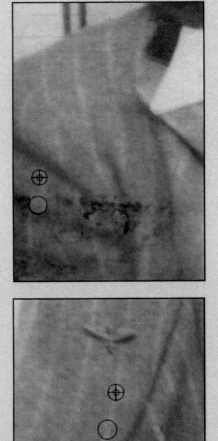

you still don't want a line between the original and the patched. With our American patriot, I did some patching in the top part, where the texture is pretty uniform.

In patching, you make a quick selection around your destination, (the damaged area) drag it to the source location, and Photoshop makes a patch out of it, placing it neatly atop your destination, and blending your edges seamlessly. Here's how:

1. Choose your Patch tool (under the Healing Brush tool).

2. Check Destination in the options bar.

3. Draw a rough selection around the bad area.

4. Check Source and drag the selection to the good part you want to use for your patch.

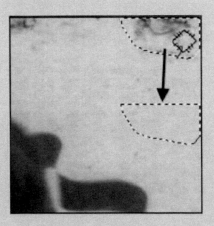

Patch tool

The **Patch** tool is new as of Photoshop version 7. It is useful when you have a relatively large area of homogeneous color and texture. The Patch tool is like a large healing tool. Like the healing tool, it uses mathematical algorithms to "fit itself" into your photo. This can be a real advantage, when your color changes are subtle, but

4

And there you are! Patched! CTRL/⌘-D to deselect the area.

> You can also use the Patch tool in reverse:
>
> - Select Source in the Options Bar.
> - Outline your source area.
> - Choose Destination in the Options bar.
> - Drag that patch around to various places that need to be patched.
> - This technique is a wee bit like having a custom brush that will magically blend in with your picture!

Sample painting

In a restoration job like this, once you have done all of the healing, patching, and cloning that you can, there are often some areas that still require a bit of painting. In this jacket, for example, over to the left side of the image, there are folds that are not similar to any that are unmarred in this photo. We probably could find suitable areas from which to clone, but often, as is the case here, it is actually easier to paint the jacket back in.

For this, I used **sample painting** as follows:

1. Always do your painting on a new layer, rather than your working copy of your photo. If you are doing quite a bit of painting, or more than one color or texture, it is generally wise to use more than one layer. Tossing out a layer or correcting on one layer is far easier than trying to correct on a complex layer with lots of colors and different

types of painting.

2. Choose an appropriate brush – probably a small soft-edged one is best for this sort of job.

3. Hold your brush over an area that has a shade of color you would like to use for painting.

4. Hold down the ALT/OPT key and your brush turns to your Eyedropper tool and with a click makes the color under the pointer the foreground (painting) color.

5. Zoom in until you can see the pixel detail.

6. Paint.

7. Keep your other hand close to that ALT/OPT key and keep sampling, painting, sampling, painting, until you have your area painted as you would like.

> When you are painting something that has complex textures, like this jacket, you will want to zoom in, sample frequently, and use small brush strokes.

Don't be intimidated by the notion of painting. If you zoom in far enough, you can see that this is just pixels! Many people have trouble painting people, because they are looking at eyes and noses and mouths, instead of at the pixels. Zooming in very closely depersonalizes your subject, making it easier to work on them. You will notice, though, that tiny differences at pixel level can actually make a difference in a person's appearance, especially in their eyes. One fix for this is to always use subtle colors sampled from the photo.

Another technique that you will find useful as you are sample painting is this: As you are zoomed in working very close, it is a good idea to consult the 100% magnification, as well. To see this, while you are working, choose **Window > Documents > New Window***. It updates in real time as you paint on your zoomed view! And always paint on a new layer. Then if you don't like what you have done, you can correct it by erasing and redoing, by masking parts, by adjusting the opacity of the layer, or by changing the layer's blending mode. If you really don't like what you have painted, you can toss that layer into the trash, make another layer, and start over! No risk.*

For this restoration, I would suggest you use sample painting on the left side of the canvas on her jacket, and on the star and stripe that are badly faded at the top. It will also come in useful, along with a few other tricks, as we start work on her eyes.

Eyes

Our subject's eyes are far too washed-out. Her left eye, in particular, has a faded whitish area in the lower left, which is, in a way, hardly noticeable, but actually imparts a disconcerting wall-eyed look to her.

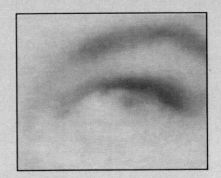

1. Make a new layer.

2. Zoom in to pixel level and look at the part of her eye that you like. See all the shades of gray? This is what "texture" is. Just pixels in varying colors!

3. Zoom in very closely and sample-paint her iris back the way we imagine it had been. Sample several times from similar areas.

4. For her pupils, make another new layer above your working layer.

5. Choose a hard round brush of a similar size to the pupil, select black as your foreground color, and touch it in about the place you want the pupils. Move them to where they belong, using the Move tool, and the arrow keys.

6. Use the Blur tool (the water droplet below the eraser) to soften them, making them fit this portrait.

7. For the catch-lights, again, make a new layer above the pupil layer.

8. Paint a little arc of white over each pupil and then blur with Gaussian blur or the Blur tool. Move these too, if you need to.

I love the way this process transformed her eyes, leaving them very sweet and soft.

4

Final touch-ups

There are some other small areas that need to be fixed, in order to complete this restoration. Toward the left side of the canvas, where the strings are, there are some troubling horizontal lines that begin there and cut right across our subject's face. One cuts right below her eyes. The others go over her cheeks level with her mouth.

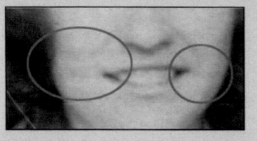

1. These can be fixed most expeditiously with the Clone Stamp tool, sampling often, using a very small brush, and zooming in and out to monitor your progress.

> Use CTRL/⌘-SPACE and click to zoom in, without losing your current tool. To zoom out, without losing your current tool, ALT/OPT-SPACE click. CTRL/⌘-+ and CTRL/⌘- - also work.

2. Use the Dodge tool, with a large soft brush, to lighten up the area along the bottom of the picture.

3. Similarly, a delicate touch with the Burn tool will darken places that are too light, such as this patch of photo-fade near her eye.

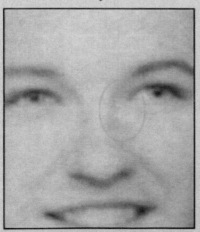

It is easiest to get a smooth result with these tools if your brush is larger than you think you need it, it is soft-edged, and you use a gentle touch.

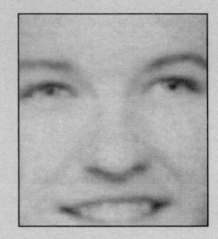

Returning some color to the photo

Finally, when we are finished with these corrections and adjustments, it is time to add some color back into the photo. Though the photo is pretty washed-out and faded, we can still tell that it had some color to it. In the next chapter, we will go through how to do a duotone process, but for now, we will stick to a single color, in trying to recreate the likely appearance of the original. Here's one way to decide what color to use.

1. By using the Eyedropper on the original, take a color sample.

2. Click on the foreground color that you just sampled and see what color family this is. By sampling a few parts of the original photo, I discerned some orange hue and some green.

3. You may need to use some artistic license here, in deciding what color to use. I would suggest that the green might be just the effect of fading, and that the original photo was more of the brown from the orange family.

4. With the top layer in the Layers palette selected, add yet another adjustment layer, this time Hue/Saturation. Check the Colorize box.

This will make all the grays in your photograph assume different values of the same color.

5. In order to make sure that your color is tending

toward the right one – sometimes green-brown and orange-brown can look remarkably similar – pull the saturation slider over to the right temporarily.

Slightly different colors can make a big difference in your outcome. Certainly experiment with this!

Here is the finished result.

4

A good boy

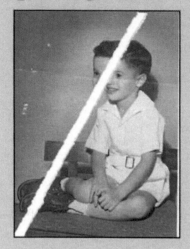

- Curves
- Healing Brush tool
- Clone Stamp tool
- Gaussian blur

4

Sometimes a photo is very badly damaged, and sometimes it is even in pieces! Although, upon first glance, this photo looks like a disaster, its repair is not very complicated. However, this work still takes patience, time, and care, if we are to do a credible job.

Bringing the two pieces together

Once we get our two pieces together, we can evaluate our situation and plan our attack.

1. As usual, start by duplicating your 'Background' layer, so you have a working layer to play with.

2. On your working layer, make a selection of one of the pieces, using whatever selection tool you deem appropriate. For this example, a Magnetic Lasso works fine.

3. Use CTRL/⌘-SHIFT-J to cut the piece off and make it into its own layer.

4. Press V to switch to the Move tool and move your cut piece into place. Using the arrow keys and zoom will help here. CTRL/⌘-D to deselect.

5. You already have a duplicate of your original, so at this point, link your working layer and the piece you moved over with it. Use CTRL/⌘-E to merge your piece onto your working layer.

If the two pieces had been scanned separately, we would do this in a very similar way. We would open the two files and drag the selected piece of one over onto the other file.

Evaluating the problem areas

Actually, we got pretty lucky on this, because there are no big areas missing. Even though the photo was torn, the actual damage is minimal. Here are the areas to be repaired:

- The photo is (or was meant to be) a monochrome, but some of its colors have faded from the yellow-gold base to a greenish tone.
- There are the gouges on the upper left side.
- There are a few dust spots to be fixed.
- Significant repair is needed on the cracks that run across the photo:
    - on the wall,
    - through his shadow on the wall,
    - on the bench,
    - on his shoes,
    - through his hair, and
    - across his facial features.

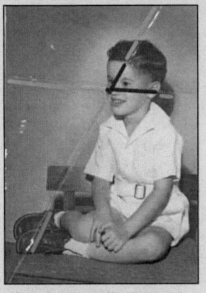

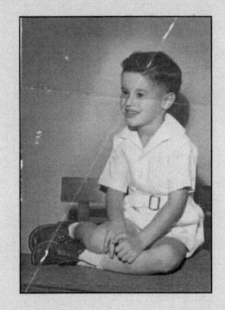

4

Tone and contrast adjustments

1. First, desaturate this photo, using **Image > Adjustments > Desaturate** .

Since it is a monochrome, any other colors that may have been scanned in will just serve as noise and will get in the way of our work. This includes that funny greenish cast.

2. We also need to adjust the contrast here a wee bit, though it is pretty good already. Apply a slight S-curve.

A time to heal

Much of what ails this photo – the gouges, dust, and much of the scratch damage – can be fixed with the Healing Brush tool.

Remember, you need to watch for infection, or invasion of a nearby color, when healing. To prevent this, while working on an area that contrasts in color with something next to it, use a selection as shown here.

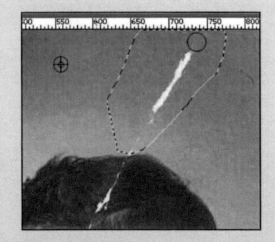

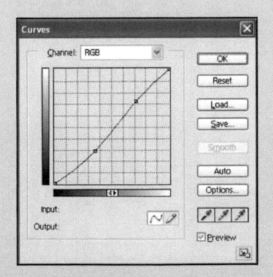

Here is what this infection looks like, if you do not isolate the target with your selection tool – you get this funny spray-paint effect, as the program tries to average out the correction into the surrounding area.

4

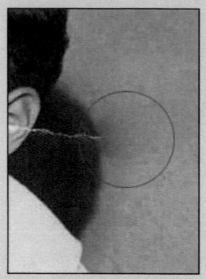

As you can see here, using a selection eliminates this problem.

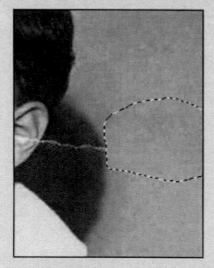

For a straight area like this photo's edge, you can use the Rectangular Marquee to select the area.

If your first try yields uneven results, often it helps to go over it again, using the same source.

Cloning to repair the big problems

While cloning used to be the best answer for many little problems, like dust and scratches, with the advent of Photoshop 7's Healing Brush tool, we have more methods to choose from. However, there are still places where the Clone Stamp tool is a good choice. It takes some practice to determine which tools are best used in particular circumstances, but in general, the Healing Brush tool will work better only when there is not much detail in the image.

One example is in the little boy's face.

1. Make a new layer above your working layer and label it 'cloning work'.

2. Select the Clone Stamp tool.

3. Check Use All Layers in the options bar.

4. Zoom in and work on this up close. Take care of the pixels, and the picture will take care of itself!

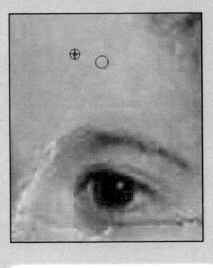

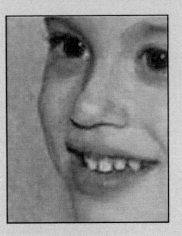

4

> When you are doing close-in zoomed work, it is a good idea to keep a zoomed-out New View open at the same time. Remember to use **Window > Documents > New Window** so you can see the effects of your changes in the big picture right away.

6. To smooth and soften this effect, duplicate the cloning work layer. Then run the duplicate through a **Filter > Blur > Gaussian Blur** of 4.4 pixels.

5. Sample often and use a small brush.

When working with detailed subjects, I prefer to clone with a hard brush, because I often don't like that fuzzy look that you can get with the soft brush. However, with facial features and diffuse areas like this background, you will likely get better results by using a soft brush.

When you are finished with a big cloning operation like this one, sometimes you can end up with a choppy, almost painted look.

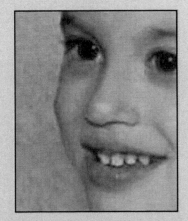

7. The original photo was a monochrome, but not desaturated, so we need to add some color back to it. To determine the original hue, use the sampling method that was detailed in the Patriot example above.

8. Adding a Hue/Saturation adjustment layer with a Hue setting of 49 and Saturation of 11 (with Colorize checked) yielded this final result.

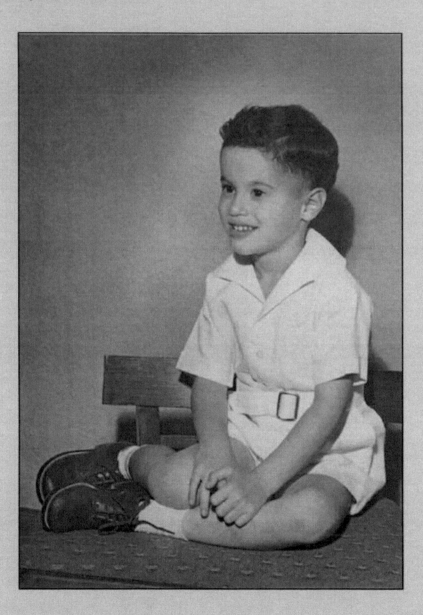

New baby

- Levels
- Gradient masking
- Adjustment layers

In this example, the bottom half of the image is badly faded, while the top is less faded. How should we attack this?

As with any project in Photoshop, there are certainly several good ways to do this, but here is one way that might come in useful in your own projects.

1. Add a Levels adjustment layer and adjust the levels till the bottom part of the photo looks like it is in good contrast.

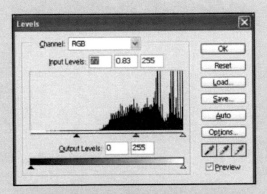

4

The top has now become too dark. We need to reduce the effect of the mask for the top half of the photo, whilst maintaining its effect toward the bottom.

2. Select the Levels adjustment layer we have just created.

3. Switch to the default foreground and background colors (press D), select the Gradient tool and ensure it is set to Linear Gradient.

4. Holding down SHIFT to ensure a vertical line, click at the top of the image and drag to the bottom, creating a gradient in the mask.

At this point, the coloring looks really off, but the contrast is evened up, as the adjustment layer has more effect on the bottom of the photo than the top, evening the fade.

5. Add a Hue/Saturation adjustment layer. Check Colorize and give the photo a nice authentic 1915 hue. Sepia would look good here, but I used a setting of 45 for Hue and 14 for Saturation, giving it a brown-gray tone that I like.

This was a really badly damaged photo and is well over 100 years old. I can't restore the bottom part to "perfection" without doing a lot more work, but the point here is to show you a method of fixing uneven fade. A bit of a touch of the healing brush on that scratch across Mr. Jackson's shoes (see the first two examples for how-tos on this), and here is the finished result!

He's my dad

- Curves
- Blending modes
- Levels
- Healing Brush tool
- Unsharp mask
- Burn and Dodge tools

This photo presents a restoration challenge. Many years of desk drawers left this photo in this condition, unevenly faded and scratched. Time also took its toll by leaving the photo with a funny greenish cast, which we will change, as well. However, the original photo could be improved, too!

The contrast between the lightness of the little boy's shirt and his face, and the darkness of the rest of the photo, left Dad almost unrecognizable. So, while we are here, we will do that work too. Though fixing the lighting is not precisely restorative in this instance, these methods can be used in bringing back discolored areas of photos we are restoring.

Because of the lack of image information available in the under-exposed parts of the photo, it is impossible to get a perfect result, but we can certainly improve upon what we are given. If I were doing this for a client, I would suggest a locket portrait, with the faces focused in an oval vignette.

Tonal corrections

Correcting the tones on a photo as badly toned as this one is often will bring out lots of detail that was not at all evident when we began. That is one reason to do these corrections first. Because of the different correction needs of the different areas of the photo, we cannot make global corrections here and expect miracles. Instead, we will do spot corrections using adjustment layers and layer masks. Please don't let these terms scare you! These babies are what make Photoshop special! If you stick with this, and go step-by-step, you can learn to

do real magic with these great tools.

1. Begin by duplicating your layer and saving the file in psd format.

2. Then desaturate the photo by adding a Hue/Saturation adjustment layer and pulling the Saturation slider to the far left.

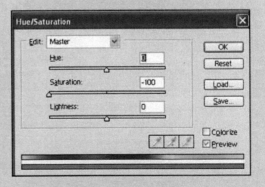

3. Some overall curves work is in order to get us in the right ball park. Then we will evaluate where we are from there. This took a bit of experimentation, but I think that this is about the best that can be done with a global curves adjustment.

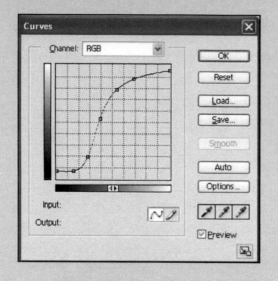

4

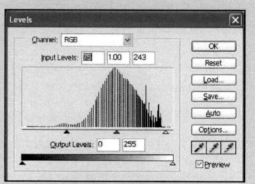

To quickly see the effects of each of the blending modes, double-click on the layer blending mode arrow, or on the Normal that appears at the top of the Layers palette. Then you can scroll through these using the up and down arrows!

4. Change the blending mode for this curves adjustment layer to Overlay. I experimented with this and think it gives the best result.

You can intensify, lessen, or otherwise change the effects of your adjustment layers using layer blending modes! This is a good reason to use them whenever you get a chance.

5. Next, let's bring out the little boy's contrast using Levels. Move the sliders so that his face is a bit darker, and his features stand out. For now, we're ignoring the rest of the photo.

Now the little boy is looking better, but Dad is far too dark, as is most of the rest of the photo. To fix this, we can use that layer mask that comes with our Levels adjustment layer!

6. Click the mask in the Layers palette. (Note that the brush that is normally in the second column of the Layers palette, beside the eye, has changed into a layer mask icon, telling you that you are about to work on the mask, not the layer.)

I find it easier to paint the part that I want to keep, using the adjustment layer, rather than painting in the background.

7. Type D to make your colors the defaults (black and white are the only colors you'll need on a mask).

8. Then ALT/OPT-BACKSPACE to fill the adjustment layer mask with black. This effectively blocks the adjustment layer.

9. Choose a feathered airbrush that is pretty large, 75-100 pixels diameter.

10. Type X to switch between your colors.

11. Paint over the little boy, and any other parts that are too dark, with your white brush.

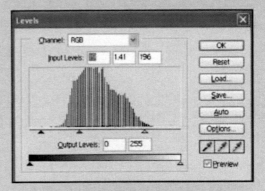

13. Now, as we did with the first Levels layer, fill the mask with black and then paint lightness into Dad's face.

Dad is still in the shadow. Let's brighten him up.

12. Using another Levels adjustment layer, bring Dad's face up so that it looks more in line with his son's. Again, ignore the rest of the photo. It will get very light, as you see here:

105

Your Layers palette should now look like this:

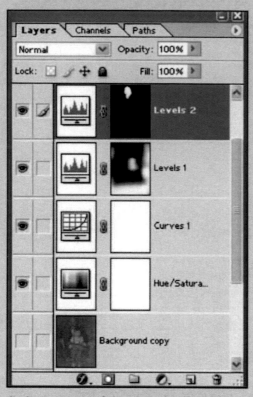

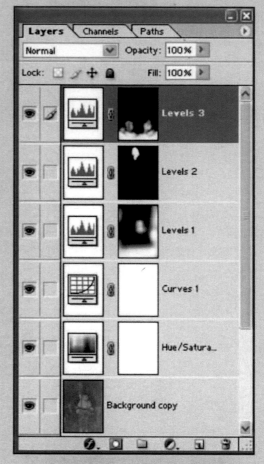

But, the bottom part of the photo is still too light.

14. Add one more Levels adjustment layer. After you have made the adjustment, again, only looking at the bottom part of the photo, fill your layer mask with black and paint in the parts that need lightening, with your soft airbrush.

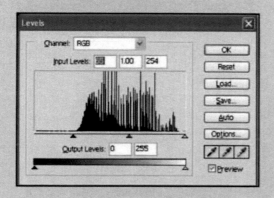

4

Removing dust and scratches

Now that we can see these people better, we can rid the photo of the scratches and creases that mar it.

1. Duplicate your 'Background' layer copy again.

2. Using the Healing Brush tool and a zoom of 200%, sample, heal, and repeat, till you have as much perfection as you can stand.

3. Going to **Filter > Sharpen > Unsharp Mask** with a value of 50% and between 1 and 2 pixels will further bring out the detail.

4. Finally, as a finishing touch, take the Burn tool and touch it to the boy's jawline and to his features, just to bring them out a bit more.

5. A bit of Dodge to the shadow on Dad's forehead works well here.

Color

We are still not quite finished! This photo is still unsaturated. Because of the fading from the years, it is impossible to tell exactly how this photo was colored originally. By looking at other pictures of the time and using some artistic license, we can come up with a color.

1. Above all the other layers, add yet another adjustment layer, this time for Hue/Saturation, click Colorize, and find a color to apply to your photo. I chose this delicious warm brown.

Again, the photograph was very badly damaged to start with, and although it is not absolutely perfect, the improvement is immense.

Wedding day

- Dust & Scratches filter
- Dodge tool
- Healing Brush tool
- Adjustment layers
- Curves and Hue/Saturation

Olive Jackson, all dressed up on her wedding day in 1884, needs very little help in this picture. A few specks of age-old dust, and a blob of grime on her starched lace collar are the main detractions. Then an adjustment of Curves to improve the contrast a bit, and a Hue/Saturation adjustment and she is as good as... old!

When I began this, I decided to preserve the coloring of the photo in order to leave myself more options as the restoration evolved.

1. For the first step, as always, duplicate your 'Background' layer so you have a working layer.

   To remove large areas of speckles, where there is background, or where detail is not important, we can use **Filter > Noise > Dust & Scratches**. This filter works a bit like the blur-painting that we did previously in the Patriot example, to remove small imperfections. It does a better job at maintaining the line between contrasting colors, but it is still best to select the area in which you want to work.

2. Make a selection, then go to **Select > Feather** and feather your selection by several pixels so that the line between filtered and not is not obvious.

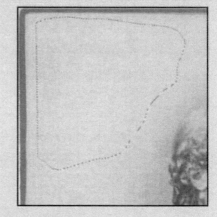

3. Go to **Filter > Noise > Dust & Scratches**. The Threshold level lets you specify how sensitive you want the filter to be. The Radius setting allows you to tell the size of the fix. Use the preview window to check your results as you adjust these settings.

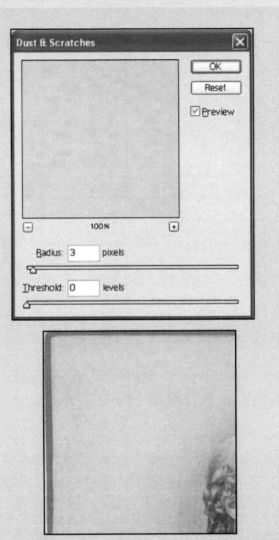

5. The rest of the goo can be removed using the Healing Brush tool on selected areas, keeping the areas with different colors distinct.

Although there are some adjustments one can make in the dialog box, I find the Dust & Scratches filter is very limited and quite difficult to control. For large dusty or scratched areas that have little important detail, it is potentially useful, but for Olive herself, it seems like using a chainsaw to trim a houseplant! I prefer using the Healing Brush tool, in little strokes, on a duplicate layer in this photo. This preserves the delicate texture of the background, too.

4. This grime on Olive's collar and neck area is the worst damage that the years have done to this photo. The darkness of the dirt on the collar can be solved by gentle application of the Dodge tool, using a soft brush.

6. Add a gently-sweeping S-curve in a Curves adjustment layer to bring out the detail.

4

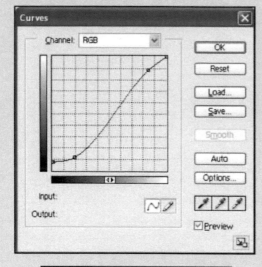

And here, in our resulting image, she is as beautiful as she was that day!

When I began this project, I preserved the coloring of the photo in order to leave myself more options as the restoration evolved. Looking through other photos from this era, including that of her husband, taken the same day, tells me that this yellowing is a result of aging, albeit very even!

7. A colorizing Hue/Saturation layer removes that yellow cast, but keeps the rich brown tones in this photo.

4

Chapter 5
Toning and Aging Images

Whether we look at the world through rose-colored glasses, through the green haze of envy, or see things in black and white, we are profoundly influenced by colors and the ways they are combined. Even a very simple photo can develop an air of mystery, wonder, or high-quality art if it is given certain color toning. As we will explore in this chapter, sometimes a color change is all we need in order to change a simple photo to a really amazing work of art!

As a photographer, you tone your photos in the darkroom with chemicals. In Photoshop, we can create the same effects, but without the fumes! On the canvas of Photoshop, we can move beyond traditional darkroom techniques, coming up with effects that we had never dared to experiment with.

And, by doing this work in Photoshop, instead of in the darkroom, your only expense is your time. Pixels are easily renewed with a click of CTRL/⌘-Z or a flick of the eraser, so there is no risk. Now you can set your creativity free – don't be afraid to experiment!

In this chapter, we will look at several ways to tone photos. First we are going to use a duotone to give some different looks to pair of baby elephants. We will then use gradients and gradient maps in new ways to stylize a photo. Next we'll have a look at aging a photo by using a sepia tone, adding dust and scratches, and even simulate tearing and burning its edges!

Finally, we will take a short look at Grunge Art. This popular style is done with many effects combined, but much of it involves color modes and blending. Grunge artists give us unusual and unexpected colors, setting the work on its edge, surprising us, and maybe shocking us a bit. Photoshop and the digital canvas is the ideal medium for creating this type of art, and we will examine some grunge color tricks at the end of the chapter.

Elephant buddies

- Duotones
- Curves

5

For this example, we will take this duo of elephant babies and make them a duotone! A duotone can make a handsome two tone photo, giving it depth and dimension, without adding much color. For example, many of Ansel Adams' black and white photo prints were actually duotones, using black and warm gray. A duotone could also be a very stylized photo with lots of color. We will look at these styles and some ways to use them effectively with your photos. Later, we will talk more about this color mode and how it works.

Always begin by saving your file with a new name. This will effectively make a copy of your file, so that your original photo remains untouched by the ravages of duotoning. To do this, open `two.tif`, go to **File > Save As...** and pick a reasonable location and filename for your new file. Save it in psd format.

Saving your working document in psd format ensures that any layers generated will be preserved later when you save. This format also protects your file from the degeneration which occurs in saving to some file formats. For example, each time you save a file in JPEG format, you are asked what quality level you want. This is so that Photoshop knows how much of the image information to get rid of in order to save at the filesize you want. Therefore, saving and resaving to JPEG format will successively degrade more of your photo details with each save. This characteristic of JPEG is called "lossiness." PSD, GIF, or TIF files are not lossy, but they have other limitations. PSD is probably the best format in which to save a working document in Photoshop.

Contrast

If your photo needs to be adjusted, this is the first thing we should attend to. In this example, we need to alter the contrast using a Curves adjustment layer.

1. To make an adjustment layer, click the Create new fill or adjustment layer button at the bottom of the Layers palette, and choose Curves.

    The steeper any part of a curve, the greater is the contrast for the represented tonal range.

2. In this example, we want more contrast in the midtones. Increase our contrast by bringing one of the lighter midtone points a bit lower and one of the darker midtone points a bit higher. This makes a gentle S-curve, as shown below.

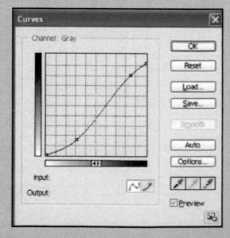

This sort of adjustment is one that you will use often in your work. Of course, to keep things exciting, each photo will require different fixes!

Next, we will convert our photo to grayscale mode. Then we can adjust the contrast further, if needed, and from there, make our duotone.

3.   To convert the photo to Grayscale mode, click **Image > Mode...** and check **Grayscale**. If you have layers, it will ask you if you want to flatten them. With other images, you might not have to flatten, but they warn that grayscaling could affect the composition of the layers. In particular, if you have used layer blending modes or color adjustment layers, changing the mode will change how these layers react. In this case, you will have to flatten your image first, so click Merge. If it asks if you want to discard color information, yes, you do. That is the whole point of grayscaling a photo.

5

Another way to make a grayscale photo, which is often better than simply using **Image > Mode > Grayscale**, *is to use Channel Splitting. In each RGB photo, you actually have four images, and these are in your channels. There is a channel that describes the red information in the photo, one for green, and one for blue. It all combines, then, to make the fourth channel which is the combination of the R, the G, and the B.(If your image is in CMYK mode, you will have 5 channels total, one each for C, M, Y, and K, and another that is the composite.)*

In channel splitting, you are going to examine the component channels of the image. This is useful in grayscaling, because often the different channels have very different contrast levels, so you can choose the one you like best. Also, it is likely that one of the channels will have more noise in it, and ridding the image of that color information in particular will often be all you need to fix that. Whilst removing color information, though, keep in mind that that is what we are doing. In removing color information, we have to watch that we are maintaining the level of detail the image demands. This is how this is done:

1. First, Ctrl/⌘-S to save. This process will use your image to split, and so it will be gone from your desktop. Any changes you make between your last save and your channel split will be gone if you do not save.

2. Flatten your image.

3. Click on the Channels tab. To the upper right on that palette, click the pop up arrow.

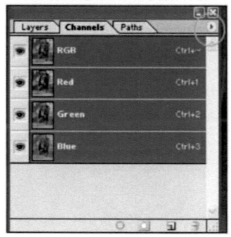

4. Upon clicking this arrow, you will see choices, one of which is Split Channels. Click that.

5. Before your eyes, your image will change to three new grayscale images, one representing each channel.

6. It is likely that one channel will stand out as having better contrast. Perhaps another will have some undesirable noise or other defect. Choose your favorite of these, and save it with a new name.

7. If you need more contrast in your image, make a Levels adjustment layer by clicking on the Add a new adjustment layer button at the bottom of the Layers palette. Use the sliders to improve its contrast, and then proceed!

5

4. To get to the Duotone Options box, click on **Image > Mode > Duotone**. Up at the top, for type, choose Duotone from the drop-down. Pick whichever mode you want from the drop-down. By clicking on each of the color chips, you can choose your own color combinations. (Click the Custom button in the Color Picker, if you need Pantone or other color collections.)

Photoshop also offers a handy collection of tried-and-true combinations of colors that you can access by clicking the Load button in that box.

> In order to get full saturation of your colors when printing, have your darkest color at the top in your Duotone Options box.

Duotone curves

The curve to the left of each color is a thumbnail of the actual curve you have set for the color. This curve enables you to adjust the amount of ink that will be used in place of the shades of gray. The box works just like the regular Curves dialog box in Photoshop, the transition between shades represented by a straight line that can be shaped to alter the tone of the image.

Duotone Curve		
0: 0.6 %	60: 51.3 %	
5: %	70: %	
10: %	80: %	
20: %	90: %	
30: 92.5 %	95: %	
40: %	100: 91.3 %	
50: %		

If you make a change in a dialog box like this and don't like it, you don't have to cancel it, bring it up again, and start over. If you hold down ALT/OPT, your Cancel button turns into Reset.

Duotone Options

Type: Duotone

Ink 1: PANTONE Process Black C

Ink 2: PANTONE Hexachrome Cyan C

OK / Reset / Load... / Save... / ☑ Preview

Overprint Colors...

Examples

Here are some examples of duotone effects you can make:

Duotone Options

Type: Duotone

Ink 1: Black

Ink 2: PANTONE 144 CVC

OK / Reset / Load / Save / ☑ Preview

Overprint Colors...

5

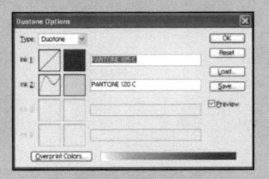

Overprint Colors is for more advanced setting of colors when exact color replication is required in printing.

At the top of the Duotone Options box, it reads "Duotone," but if you click the drop-down, you see also options for Tritone and Quadtone. You handle these just as you did duotones – you just have 3 or 4 colors at work in your photo instead of two.

What's going on here? In a duotone image, the curves adjustments you make determine how the two colors of ink will be distributed over the image. You could make it so that one color is applied as a tint to the highlights (lighter tones), while the other is used mainly to tint the shadows (darker tones), for example. With a Tritone or Quadtone image, the third (and fourth) color can be used on another part of the image, perhaps the midtones, potentially adding even more interest and dimension to the photo.

If you land on a duotone setting that you particularly like, or one that you would like to have available to use again, save it by clicking Save on the Duotone Options box.

Here is a wild combination that might make a good CD cover:

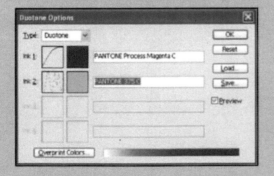

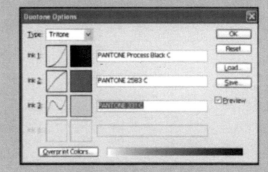

5

5

Playing with the dog

- Gradient maps
- Layer blending modes
- Adjustment layers

In this section, we will be working with gradient maps and ways to combine them with blending modes and adjustment layers. That is, if you want to call it work – as far as I'm concerned manipulating colored layers with layer blending modes is just plain fun! I suppose one could calculate in advance what would happen if you took a blue / yellow gradient layer and blended it using difference mode with a red / green gradient layer. But perhaps the best way to get an idea about the possible effects is by playing around and experimentation. We will look at some of these ideas in this example.

In looking at the choices for adjustment layers, you have seen that there are more adjustment possibilities than Hue/Saturation, Levels, and Curves. In fact, there is a raft of possibilities, one of which we will look at here – applying a Gradient Map. In a gradient map, you choose or make a gradient whose colors link up and identify with the tonal values in your picture.

For example, in this picture of Maddy, when we apply the red-white-blue gradient, the red is mapping onto the light areas, the blue onto the dark, and the white to the midtones. Let's look at how this works:

1. Click on the Add adjustment layer button at the bottom of the Layers palette and choose Gradient Map.

2. In the Gradient Map window, click the drop-down arrow to the right of the gradient. This will give you the pre-loaded gradients. You can add more by clicking on the drop-down arrow in the pre-loaded gradients box. There are some collections from which to choose at the bottom of that list. You can reverse the gradient, as I have done, by checking the Reverse box.

3. You can make your own gradient by clicking on the colored window in the Gradient Map dialog. This brings up the Gradient editor. Click anywhere along the bottom of the gradient to add another color stop. Choose your color by clicking the color square at the bottom. Slide the color stops around to get different proportions for your gradient. When you get one you like and want to keep, click New.

4. Once you have your gradient as you like it, click OK.

5

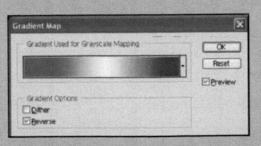

Masking a gradient map adjustment layer

One special advantage to working with adjustment layers in Photoshop is your ability to mask them. Notice that the adjustment layer in the Layers palette has a built-in mask. Click on that, choose a black brush, and paint Maddy's original blackness back in!

Here, I have left it looking as if she had walked in a tray of blue paint, which I know that she would do, given the opportunity.

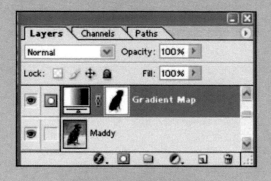

We can fade the color into the photo, in this way, by dragging a black to white gradient across the mask. For the effect in this example, I dragged a Linear gradient from the lower left corner to the upper right. The gradient styles, Linear, Radial, Angle, Reflected, or Diamond, are in the Gradient Options box toward the left. Try each of these to get a feeling for what they do.

Amazing gradients

Yet another exciting thing to do with color is what I term "Amazing Gradients". This is what happens when you mix gradient layers together in different ways using layer blending modes. You can spend a good deal of time on these, not because they are particularly difficult to do, but because they are fun! The various blending modes affect gradient layers in often surprising ways. From this play, you reap the added reward of enough experience with the blending modes that you get some understanding for the sort of things that they do.

To apply a gradient layer with a blending mode to our photo of Maddy, we proceed like this:

1. Click the Add a new layer icon at the bottom of the Layers palette.

2. Choose the Gradient tool (It might be hidden under the Paint Bucket.).

3. Choose two different colors for your foreground and background colors in your Color Picker.

4. In the Gradient Options bar, choose one of the gradient styles: Linear, Radial, Angle, Reflected, or Diamond.

5. Drag your Gradient tool across your new layer. If you want to constrain your gradient to an increment of 45°, hold the SHIFT key as you drag. Your picture is now covered by this gradient layer.

6. In the Layers palette, near the top is the drop-down for the layer blending modes.

5

example, you could use a gradient map with the corporate colors in a creative photo layout. A duotone photo can make good use of the two colors already being employed in printing the client's brochure. And an Amazing Gradient could give you a wowza backdrop for a greeting card design!

PC users: If you click once on the word "Normal," you will see a drop-down with all of the modes listed. If you click again, your "Normal" becomes highlighted. When this happens, you can use your arrow keys to scroll through the blending modes! Flip through them till something strikes you as cool but, be warned, this will fill your History palette pretty fast.

7. Add another layer.

8. Put another gradient in it, a different kind, or different colors.

9. Flip through the blending modes for that layer.

10. Repeat as desired.

11. You can add layers of custom gradients, pictures, objects, solid colors, patterns, or anything.

Examples

This technique provides a fertile ground for your creativity. Here are some done with Maddy. In each of the Layers palettes here, the blending mode used for the layer is the name of the layer. The 'Gradient Map 1' you see in some of the Layers palettes is this:

As you look through these and work with these techniques, I hope you will be thinking of ways to incorporate these creative techniques into your "real" work. For

5

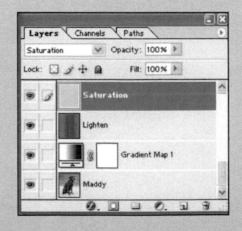

End-of-reel effects
Open a new version of `maddy.tif`.

Let's have a look at how to achieve this cool end-of-reel effect in the image below.

1. First add a gradient map, with the settings I showed you at the start of the examples section.

2. Then click on the Create a new layer icon at the bottom of the Layers palette. In that layer add a red / violet Reflected gradient.

3. When the image disappears, remain calm. With the new gradient layer selected in the Layers palette, change the layer blending mode to Lighten. Cool, eh?

4. Then we can finish off this look by adding another new layer atop the gradient layer. Fill this layer with yellow and apply a Saturation blending mode to it.

5

The Tulip Trestle

- Adjustment layers
- Masking
- Gaussian blur
- Airbrush tool
- Burn tool
- Noise filter
- Unsharp mask
- Pen tool

5

It seems as if we are always trying for what we don't have. If our photo is old, we want it to look new. If our photo is new, we want it to look old!

In this example, we start with a May 2002 digital photo of the Tulip Trestle, in Tulip, Indiana, USA. We will make it look as if it had been taken in May of 1907, the year after the trestle was built. This is, incidentally, the longest single-span railroad trestle in the United States, and the second longest in the world. (The longest is in Germany.) In order to get that authentic old-photo look, let's:

- Add sepia toning.
- Edge the photo.
- Add dust and scratches.
- Add smudges and smears.
- Make a 1900s-style title.
- Mount the photo.

Protect your work

Before you do any work to your photo at all, **File > Save As ..** and give your file a new name. Save it in psd format and put it somewhere where you will be able to find it later. As you progress, press CTRL/⌘-S periodically to save your work.

Add sepia toning

There are probably several ways to tone a photo with sepia, including using Photoshop's built-in action for sepia toning. Because I like to have better control over my result, I generally prefer the brute force approach. I like to make my own sepia tone using my own settings in a Hue/Saturation adjustment layer.

To make this layer above the original image, click on the Add adjustment layer button at the bottom of the layers palette. Choose Hue/Saturation.

I realize that there is a built-in action for sepia toning, but I would never use that. Old-time photos were not all some universal "sepia" color. Sepia varies from photo to photo, depending on how they are stored, the lab which processed them, and many other factors. I encourage you to move the sliders around and find your own favorite sepia. Here are my favorite settings for sepia toning – at least for this photo:

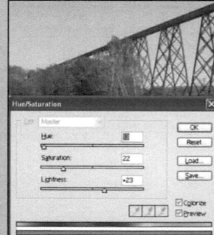

Another reason I'm not a massive fan of Photoshop's built-in action is this – older photos often tend to be either under-exposed or over-exposed, as photo equipment and developing methods were not as sophisticated as they are now. So, to create authentic old-looking photos, we want to avoid the perfection that the built-in action achieves. This setting of mine makes the image a little bit too light, which looks right for the subject on this spring day.

Edging the photo

There are many ways to effectively edge a photo to give it an authentically old look, but first we have to put it onto a larger canvas. We can do that one of two ways:

- You could extend the canvas on which you are working. To do this, begin by making your photo into a regular layer by double-clicking it in the Layers palette. Then go to **Image > Canvas Size ...** and increase the size of the canvas.

- You could drag the image to a new file.

For this image, we want to make a border for the photo and save it as a file that we can use to border other photos of the same proportions. You can even make an action to place a photo into this border and batch process a whole folder to give all of them the same border. Very handy stuff!

For now, though, we will content ourselves with making one border and putting this picture into it. We will create a file for this border, however, so that you will be able to use it later, if you want to.

Some of the photos from around the turn of the last century have a sort of roughly scalloped edge, as if they were striving for a "torn" look. This is how I emulated this border:

1. Go to **File > New...** Make your new file's dimensions larger than the one on which you are working. It is better to make it too big, than not big enough. You can always crop later. The new file's mode must be the same as your photo. Your dimensions will depend upon how much border you want around your photo. Name this file "Squiggly Photo Frame," or something equally clever. If you are only going to use this for web work, then 72 ppi is perfect. But if you think that you are ever going to want to print a photo using this border, make it 300 ppi.

2. **File > Save As...** Then find a suitable location in your hard drive and make a new folder that will be for picture borders. Save your psd format file there. From time to time, then, as we go through this edging of your photo, CTRL/⌘-S to save your work.

3. Type V to select the Move tool and drag your photo and its adjustment layer into your new file.

Holding the SHIFT key as you drag keeps your photo centered. After you have moved your photo to the new file, you can save and close the original file. The adjustment layer and the photo should be at the top of your Layers palette.

4. Double-click the 'Background' layer to make it into a regular layer. Double-click the name 'Background' and type 'border' for its name. In your Color Picker, choose the color you want for the border immediately around your photo. I chose my favorite ivory, #FFFAEE. (This is a hexadecimal code for this color. To get it, type the number into the # line at the bottom of your color picker and click OK.) ALT/OPT-BACKSPACE to fill your layer with the color.

5. Click the Create a new layer icon to make a layer and label it 'page'. It should be above the 'porder' layer in the Layers palette.

6. Fill the 'page' layer with whatever color and texture you want for the page on which your photo will ultimately be mounted. I used the wheat thatch paper described here.

For the wheat thatch paper used here, proceed as follows:

- Click your Color Picker and choose #FCE6E0, tan. ALT/OPT-BACKSPACE to fill your 'page' layer with it.

- **Filter > Add Noise ..** 15% Gaussian Monochromatic.

- **Filter > Brush Strokes > Crosshatch** (Settings 35, 1, 1).

5

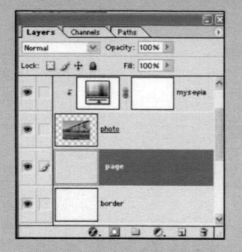

7. Type L to choose the Lasso tool and draw a random squiggly frame.

8. Now we want to cut a hole in the 'page' layer so that the 'border' layer shows through. With Photoshop, there are at least three ways to accomplish a task. This is no exception. We will use a layer mask this time.

    (If this next part seems confusing, please don't feel alone. It takes some practice with working with layer masks to get onto what it is that they do and with their amazing versatility. Read through it slowly, but don't worry about understanding what you are doing just now. Actually doing it will help you to understand it.)

    Generally, when we add a layer mask with a selection active, the selected area becomes the white part of the mask, the visible area of the layer. The rest of the mask then becomes black, making the layer invisible there. Well, we want the selected area to be black on the mask so that the layer (the wheat thatch) is not visible here.

However, if we ALT/OPT-click the Add layer mask button at the bottom of the Layers palette, we get what we want. The selection becomes the black part of the mask, making it appear as if there is a hole in the page layer, the wheat thatch.

So do that. ALT/OPT-click the Add layer mask button at the bottom of the Layers palette. This creates a layer mask with the selection area in black. You will see that mask in the Layers palette, linked to the 'page' layer. Black on the layer mask gives the effect, as you see, of cutting a hole in the page so that whatever is below it shows through!

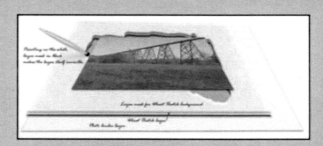

5

Next let's add a shadow to this border, to make it look as if the bordered photo is sitting atop the page. The problem lies in the fact that you need to have the shadow **above** the 'page' layer. The mask on the 'page' layer will hide the shadow if you put the shadow below it.

In this method, I use the selection that we have made for the border (the mask for the 'page' layer) to make the shadow. For the brute force method to make this shadow, proceed as follows:

1. CTRL/⌘-click on the layer mask for the 'page' layer to load it (white) as a selection. CTRL/⌘-SHIFT-I (or go to **Select > Inverse**.) makes the inverse of the mask (black) your selection.

2. Make a new layer above the others. Label it 'shadow.' Type D (default colors) and ALT/OPT-BACKSPACE to fill the selection with black. Press CTRL/⌘-D to deselect.

3. Go to **Filter > Blur > Gaussian Blur**. The size will depend upon the size of your image Here, I've used a radius of 4 pixels.

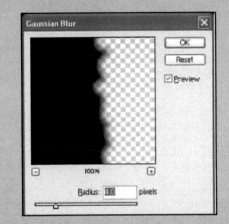

4. CTRL/⌘-click the mask on your 'page' layer again. Go to **Select > Inverse**, and then, with your shadow layer selected, tap the DELETE key. CTRL/⌘-D to deselect.

5. Use your Lasso to trace loosely around any part of the shadow that you do not want showing, (like at the top of the photo, if that is your light source) and click the DELETE key. CTRL/⌘-D to deselect.

6. Adjust the opacity if you like, by typing a number for the percent you want. Typing "5" for example, yields a shadow at 50% opacity. If you want even more control over opacity, type two numbers quickly. "85" will give you 85% opacity. (You can also use the slider in the Layers palette.)

Now you can use this frame for any photo you wish, by opening it, adding the photo of your choice, and then saving with a different name! Before you go on, if you are saving this file for use with other photos, CTRL/⌘-S to save it.

5

7. For this example, go to **File > Save As...** and name it `trestle2`. Leave it in psd format. This will make another copy of this file, leaving your original pristine.

> *You can create many different kinds of borders into which to place photos. Keep them in a folder on your machine and you will always have one at the ready.*
>
> *The above procedure for making a border, masking the 'page' layer so that the border shows through around the picture, is just one way to accomplish this. You could also have the 'border' layer on top and put a layer mask on that, so the 'page' layer shows through on the outside.*

Burned edges

1. Make the layer you want for your page, as you did above. Here I used a lavender wheat thatch paper. (For directions for wheat thatch paper, see previous).

2. Using the Lasso tool, trace around an irregular border.

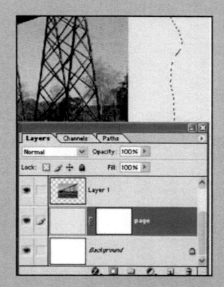

3. Hold down ALT/OPT as you click on the Add layer mask button in the Layers palette. As above, this makes the selection the black part of the layer mask, rendering that part of the layer invisible.

4. Move your photo to below the 'page' layer. (We had it on top just so we could see where to trace the border.)

5. Make a new layer between your photo and your 'page' layer.

6. Choose a warm tan (#987D53, for example) and, using a large soft airbrush, paint around on the new layer. You don't need to be neat about this, but do make sure to get all of the border covered, and don't make it too even.

7. Make another new layer atop the tan one and, using black and a smaller airbrush, color in the burned ash edge around the outside.

8. Use a soft brush with the Burn tool on the tan layer, if you need to, to make it more ... burned.

Torn edges

Sometimes a little tear gives the impression of age. It is quite possible to do this convincingly with Photoshop!

1. Begin this by making a layer of a background color that will contrast with your torn edge. I used a dark blue.

2. Add another layer containing a paper-like texture, which will be the border for your photo. For this, I used the light gray version of wheat thatch paper that was described earlier in the chapter.

3. Use your Lasso tool to select a jagged edge, as shown here.

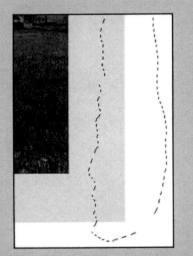

4. Hold down the ALT/OPT key and click the Add layer mask button at the bottom of the Layers palette. This adds a layer mask that hides the selected part.

5. Put a contrasting background under your photo, so you can see the edge well.

6. Click on the layer mask and choose the Smudge tool. (It is in the flyout under the Blur tool.).

7. Smudge outward in different directions so that it looks like pulled fibers. Use a fairly small brush for this and strive for randomness.

You can make the photo itself be torn instead of just the border as follows:

1. Click the 'photo' layer and type V to grab your Move tool. Now move the photo over to the torn edge. CTRL/⌘-click the layer mask for the border.

2. With the 'photo' layer selected, click the Add layer mask button.

3. Add another layer above the 'photo' layer. Choose a hard round brush and white.

4. CTRL/⌘-click on the mask for the 'photo' layer to load this as a selection.

5. With your paintbrush, paint some of the torn tips white. CTRL/⌘-D to deselect.

5

Add a layer, add a layer, add a layer... Before long, you can accumulate an unwieldy number of layers! If you are sure you are finished manipulating layers for a component of your picture, merging layers is a good way to reduce your number of layers, and also the size of your working file. To do this, begin by linking the layers you want to merge by selecting one and then clicking on the blank link box next to the eye for each of the others that you want to merge. Then CTRL/⌘-E to merge linked.

Another nifty way to manage your layers is to use Layer Sets. With a layer set, you can duplicate, move, or delete a group of layers in one step, a great time-saver! You can also add a mask to a layer set or assign an attribute such as a blending mode or an opacity level to the set. Very cool.
Here's how to put layers into a Layer Set:
Link the layers by selecting one and then clicking on the empty link box next to the eye for the each layer you want in your set.
In the Layers palette drop-down to the upper right, click on New Set from Linked.

Name the set and assign it a color, for even more organization!

Adding dust, smudges, and scratches

Dust

There is more to making a photo old than just toning it. We need some flaws like dust, smudges, and scratches. Here is a recipe for custom dust:

1. Make a new layer, name it 'dust' and fill it with a medium gray.

2. Go to **Filter > Noise > Add Noise...** Make it monochrome, Gaussian, and a setting of about 10 percent.

3. Go to **Filter > Blur > Gaussian Blur...** Make it about 3 pixels.

4. Go to **Filter > Sharpen > Unsharp Mask...** Use the maximum percentage, 500%, Radius of about 2, and Threshold of 0 Levels.

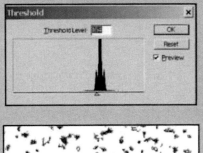

> *You can get different looks to the dust, depending upon how much blur and how much sharpening you do. You can come back and experiment at this step after you do the next one.*

5. Now this part is quite cool: **Image > Adjustments > Threshold...** Pull the slider over until you get some dust, the amount you want.

6. If you like this dust well enough that you think you would like to use the exact same dust again, you can drag this to a new file and save it. Hey, it has been done!

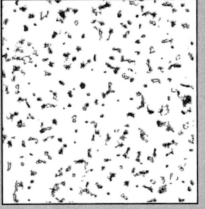

7. In the Layers palette, change the blending mode of the 'dust' layer to Multiply.

As cool as this dust is, you won't want all of it, but you can get rid of the excess in a flash.

8. With the 'dust' layer selected in the Layers palette, click the Add layer mask button at the bottom of that palette.

9. To get rid of the dust that is on the page, but not on the photo or its border, CTRL/⌘-click the mask for the 'page' layer. Now click on the 'dust' layer's layer mask. Type D to get the Default colors (black on white). ALT/OPT-BACKSPACE to fill your selected area of your mask with black. This gets rid of all the dust outside of the border. CTRL/⌘-D to deselect.

10. Choose your brush and then pick a soft airbrush in a large size, probably 100 or more pixels wide.

11. Airbrush the excess dust away.

Smudges

Make some of the "dust" into smudges, by taking the Blur tool or the Smudge tool (under the Blur tool) and smearing some of the dust. Be sure, when you are doing this, that you are smudging the LAYER and not its mask! The layer mask icon will show to the left of the thumbnail to indicate if you are working on the mask.

Using a layer mask to "erase," actually hides. This gives you the freedom to bring it back later if you want!

Scratches

For a convincing scratch, we need a curve that is smoother than one that I can do by hand, so I used the Pen tool for this one:

1. Use the Pen tool to click where you want the curve to begin, and then again where you want it to end.

2. Choose the Convert Point tool (the carat under the pen tool) and click-drag it on one of your endpoints to bend your line just a bit.

3. Create a new layer and choose a very light brown and a one-pixel brush.

4. Click on your Layers palette and then on the Stroke Path button.

5. Use an eraser at 50% opacity to erase parts of this scratch so that it isn't too uniform.

6. A bit of very conservatively-applied light tan (#F4E1C9) on a new layer between the border and the page layers completes your nicely faded border.

A very important part of making this sort of work convincing is keeping it natural. It seems to me as if nature is characterized by her randomness, perhaps more than by anything else. In Photoshop, randomness is surprisingly harder to accomplish than is regularity. For regularity, we can depend upon patterns, reiterating transformations, and other mathematically pure functions our software can help us with. For randomness, we have to rely upon our own eye to choose that which is not balanced, even, or equal.

Adding a 1900s-style title

Often, photos from the early 20th century have titles that were hand-written on the negative. To give this final touch of home-spun old-time reality, write your own caption on your old photo! Here's one way to do this: Make a new layer above all of the others.

1. Then using a brush with a Charcoal Pencil tip, closely spaced, in a light tan, (#EED2AA) write your title by hand.

2. You can experiment with different brush tips, of course, and also you may wish to try other brush dynamics. For this trestle example, I did not use dynamics.

Mount the photo

Add some corner holders, if you like. Drawing one, duplicating and flipping the layer is a good way to get uniformity among these. These corners were drawn with a hard round brush within the confines of a square selection. I added a touch of white airbrush, to give a slightly beveled effect, and a Drop Shadow to add to the 3D look.

5

5

Grunge Maddy

Color can be used to soothe us, or make us excited. It can make us want to buy certain things, or determine how well we like the taste of our food. In the case of Grunge art, at times, color can be abrasive, almost to the point of pain!

Grunge art is characterized by its anti-aesthetic nature, confusing subject matter(s), disharmonic color combinations combined with unexpected textures and broken lines, and its bizarre messages or non-messages spelt out in pieced together distressed fonts. In Photoshop, this art is created with many techniques. Among these are the use of multiple layers, blending modes, adjustment layers, and layer masks. Textures and patterns are used and abused frequently as are techniques like smudging and blurring. Our torn and burned paper effects from the Trestle example above fit in well with this art style. And so does this chapter's discussion on applying color to images!

Making Grunge art

Rather than detail all of the steps that it took to make this example piece, I will, instead, give steps for a few of the effects, and then let my Layers palette do the rest of the talking. In this Layers palette, I have labeled the layers with what they are, with the blending mode, if it is something other than normal, and the opacity, if it is other than 100%.

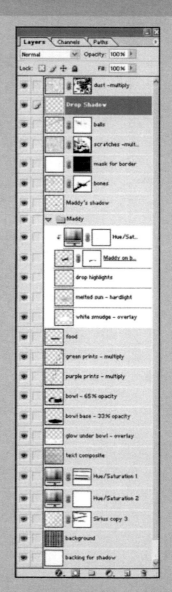

5

I began this by thinking of a topic, a message. When Grunge art is not advertising snowboards or tacos, it often covers themes like hunger or war. Keeping it light for the purposes of this book, I chose to work with the dog image, Maddy.

This project actually began as a continuation of the gradient project with Maddy. I began with the 4-color Amazing Gradient result and made it into a tiled background.

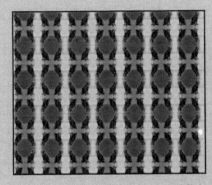

I added a Hue/Saturation layer to mute and lighten the tiled background, which was quite saturated. In the end result, you really cannot discern much of this background, except at the top. I guess it is there in spirit, though, and the composition looks very different without it!

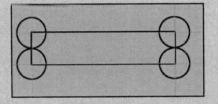

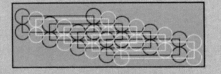

Then I began to get ideas of objects that I wanted to incorporate into the composition. The drafting-table Milkbones are stroked selections which I duplicated using an iterative transformation.

5

5

Iterative transformation

An iterative transformation is one that is repeated over and over. This is the principle upon which fractals are based. It is also a way to produce some pretty cool geometric art in Photoshop! Using layer sets is a good way to manage file size when doing this work. Here's how to do it:

1. Click the Create a new set button at the bottom of the Layers palette.
2. Click the Create a new layer button.
3. Make an object on the new layer.
4. Duplicate the layer by dragging it to the Create a new layer icon at the bottom of the Layers palette.
5. CTRL/⌘-T to bring up the Transformation box.
6. Transform your object in some way. You can rotate it, scoot it over, make it smaller, or any combination. You can do this with the handles, with arrow keys, or numerically. Click ENTER to apply the transformation.
7. CTRL/⌘-ALT/OPT-SHIFT-T and repeat as many times as you wish. What this does is to perform your transformation on a copy of the last one you did, making a new layer in the process.
8. These layers can multiply very fast, increasing your file size at the same time. To reduce your memory load, it is prudent to merge these from time to time. You can do this expeditiously if you use layer sets!

- When you are ready to merge, if you have more iterations left to go, click the Create a new set button to make a second layer set.
- Click on the topmost of your layers in the first set, the last copy you made, and drag it up to just between the first and second layer sets in your Layers palette. This will put this layer into the second set.
- Click on Set 1 (its title), and CTRL/⌘-E to merge this layer set.
- Click the layer you put up into Set 2, and CTRL/⌘-ALT/OPT-SHIFT-T anew! This will enable you to start where you left off.

I used two other iterative transformations, one for the text and another to create the ball set.

For the color-fade on the ball set, I first colored them blue using **Image > Adjust > Hue/Saturation**. Then I made a green Hue/Saturation layer for them. On the mask for that layer, I made a white / black gradient, which made the gradual green / blue blend.

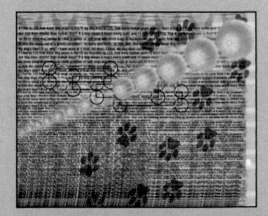

I finished this part off by adding another layer (in case I didn't like the results) and, with a small hard paintbrush using white, painted some highlights on the drips.

To make an adjustment layer apply to only the layer below it, add a clipping group. To do this, hold your pointer over the line between the adjustment layer and the one below it. Hold the ALT key and when your pointer turns into intersecting circles, click. Another slick way to do this is the keyboard shortcut. With your new adjustment layer selected in the Layers palette, type CTRL/CMD+G to Group with Previous!

Maddy was colored using a Hue/Saturation adjustment layer set to Colorize.

5

I added a layer mask to her and "cut" dents in her where she is lying in the food. I painted the shadow that appears on her on another layer, with a soft, black airbrush.

The food bowl and food were painted by hand and then the bowl layers were made translucent by adjusting their opacity in the Layers palette.

Each little component of this piece is something of a project in itself. For the lavender "sun" atop Maddy's food, for example, here's what I did:

- I began by splatting the melting lavender sun on top of the food (sun1.tif). This was one of the custom shapes that comes with Photoshop 7.

- I stylized it with some wind. (**Filter > Stylize > Wind...** Blast.. from the right).

- Then I shaped the "drips" by dragging out some parts with the Smudge tool and then shaping them with the eraser.

I need to stress at this point that this work was really extemporaneous. Mostly, I did not plan what I was going to do next. Rather, it was as if I were merely reacting to the art as it happened. When the sunshine arms reminded me of something drippy, I decided to capitalize upon that, by painting the drips and then highlighting them. It ends up making sense with the composition, too, since, when she is not lying in the sun, she likes to be out in the rain!

The tear at the bottom was done using the same method I used above for the Trestle.
I did much in this composition with layer masks – muting dust and scratches, bringing objects from lower layers in front of objects in higher layers.

Though this was not an easy project, by any stretch, and it took considerable time to compose, it was certainly fun to do. After you have gotten your feet wet with the other techniques in this chapter, assemble some ideas of your own, and have a go at grunge!

5

5

Chapter 6
Hand Coloring Techniques

A great way to make an image stand out, or bring to life an image without much or any color, is to provide that detail by hand. Traditionally this process takes a lot of practice and time, and if you make a mistake you have to start from the beginning. There is good news for people who do not want to invest the time and energy it takes to master this traditional technique and, unsurprisingly given the title of this volume, it's called Photoshop.

Hand coloring for the most part involves a lot of mouse work. If you have a graphics tablet, I recommend using it. For those of you who don't have one, get one. For those who don't even know what I'm talking about, let me enlighten you...

A graphics tablet is a pressure-sensitive surface that is used in conjunction with a pressure-sensitive pen to act as or replace a mouse. The benefits of having one at your disposal are both obvious and not so obvious.

First the obvious; better pointer control when you are doing manipulations and drawings, etc. You can take advantage of the pressure sensitivity features of Photoshop brushes. Also, if you are a left-handed person living in a right-handed mouse world (like your author), your precision and control will dramatically increase.

And the not so obvious? It can save your wrists. There mere act of switching between the mouse and the pen, using whichever is most suited to the task in hand, cuts down the risk of incurring assorted variants of Repetitive Strain Injury, including Carpal Tunnel Syndrome caused, believe it or not, by the weight of your mouse.

There are several brands of art tablet available, one of the most popular being Wacom. Their range starts remarkably cheaply but, for those weighed down by their wallets, it is even possible to buy tablets with built in screens so you're effectively working directly on your image.

All these products now have Photoshop 7 drivers, though very early in its release some of the older drivers didn't properly accommodate some of Photoshop's new brush features. Check the manufacturer's web site for updated drivers.

Okay, enough with the sales pitch, on with the Photoshop... In this chapter we will learn how to subtract color from a color image and add color to a black & white one. The easiest way to learn this is to do it, so let's jump right in!

Artificial color

- Hue/Saturation Image Adjustments
- Magnetic Lasso
- Dry Media Brushes

We are going to convert this image into a sepia tone image by using the Hue/Saturation, then add color to specific areas such as the lips, eyes and cheeks.

1. Start by duplicating the Background layer and renaming it 'Model'. Turn the visibility of the Background layer off.

2. Now with the Model Layer selected go **Image > Adjustments > Hue/Saturation** or CTRL/⌘-U on the keyboard.

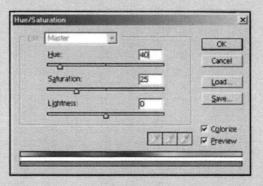

3. Click on the Colorize option to change the image to sepia tones. Adjust the Hue to around 40 to fine-tune the image to a sepia tone by getting rid of the magenta present. Leave the Saturation to where Photoshop placed it.

Now we are going to start adding color back into the model's lips, eyes and cheeks. Let's start with the lips.

4. Choose the Magnetic Lasso tool, making sure the feathering is set to around 5px. Now select the lips with the tool. You can, of course, use whichever selection tool you are happiest with.

5. Open Hue/Saturation again by choosing **Image > Adjustments > Hue/Saturation** or CTRL/⌘-U on the keyboard. Click on the Colorize option to get the color back in the lips. Set the Hue to 0, the Saturation to 30 and the Lightness to –6.

around Hue: 137. Now tone it down using the Saturation slider. I set it to around 17, effectively changing the bright green to a green-gray.

Deselect all. Your image should look similar to the one below.

6. Deselect all by pressing CTRL/⌘-D on the keyboard. So far, so good.

7. Now let's tackle the eyes. Again using the Magnetic Lasso tool, select one of the eyes. Then using the SHIFT key, add the other eye to the selection. Remember that you can keep clicking yourself with the Magnetic Lasso to add a point and guide Photoshop.

8. Again choose **Image > Adjustments > Hue/Selection**. Select the Colorize option again. Since her eyes were originally brown, converting them back doesn't leave a noticeable change. Change their color using the Hue slider. I chose a green at

The image is looking good, but let's add some color to the cheeks to finish it.

9. To do this, choose the brush tool. Open the Brushes option box and select **Load Dry Media Brushes** from the fly-out window. Select the pastel medium tip brush and set the pixel diameter to around 135. Set the Opacity to around 15% and choose the Airbrush option.

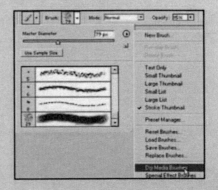

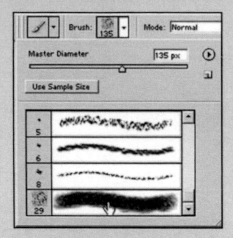

10. Now click on the Foreground color to select a new color. Choose a light pink. I've selected #F9C0C4 (R: 249; G: 196; B: 196).

11. Gently sweep the cheeks with the brush until you achieve the desired effect. It should look very subtle, like the final image opposite.

From black and white to color

- Image Modes
- Polygonal Lasso
- Layers
- Hue/Saturation Image Adjustments
- Brightness/Contrast

For this image we will color the grass and the sky, but will leave the buildings and trees in the image as they are, as the lighting and weather gives them a silhouette effect anyway. Let's start by adding some color to the grass.

1. To add color to a black and white image we first have to convert it to a color mode. **Image > Mode > RGB**. Duplicate the background layer and rename it Barn.

2. Using the Polygonal Lasso tool, set the Feather to 0px in the tool options bar, then select the grass. Use as many clicks as you feel are necessary to follow the shape of the earth.

3. We are now going to move the grass on to its own layer so that the coloring doesn't bleed into the sky area. Click **Layer > New > Layer Via Cut**. Rename the layer 'Grass'.

4. With the 'Grass' layer active use **Image > Adjustments > Hue/Saturation** or Ctrl/⌘-U on the keyboard. Turn on the colorize option and adjust the Hue slider to a shade of green that you

like. I've set the Hue to 146 and the Saturation to 25.

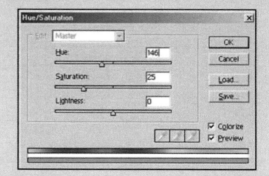

5. Now select the 'Barn' Layer. Again choose **Image > Adjustments > Hue/Saturation** (Ctrl/⌘-U) and select the colorize option. This time choose a shade of blue you like for the sky. I set the Hue to 205 and the Saturation to 23 to get a blue-gray sky.

6

6. Still on the 'Barn' layer, choose **Image > Adjustments > Brightness/Contrast**. Set the Contrast to around +25.

7. Select the 'Gras's layer and open Brightness/Contrast again. This time set the Contrast to +20.

   Turn on visibility to all layers to view the completed effect. Let's take a look at our completed image. This effect could also be achieved with adjustment layers, which would give more flexibility should you have an indecisive client.

6

6

History of art

- Hue/Saturation Image Adjustment
- History brush
- History palette

Another handy and much forgotten technique in this field is to the Art History brush. The Art History brush erases the current state of an image returning it to a point in the history that we choose.

1. Open image `flowers.tif`.

2. As usual, start by duplicating the background layer and renaming the new layer appropriately.

For this technique we will again start by turning off the color information in the image, and then return parts of it to specific areas with the History brush.

3. Choose **Image > Adjustments > Hue/Saturation**. Select the colorize option and use the Hue and Saturation slides to make the image look like a straight black and white image. I've set the Hue to 131 and the Saturation to 7.

4. Now take a snapshot of the image by clicking on the camera icon at the bottom of the History palette. By doing this we are saving a state in the history panel that we can refer back to no matter how many things we do to the image. However, once you close the image, this snapshot is not saved.

Okay, we've got our snapshot now in case we need to go back. Now we decide on the areas where we want to add the color back. I have chosen the flower in the fore-

6

ground to recolor first. I'm going to do that at full opacity and then recolor parts of the background at a lower opacity.

5. Select the History brush. (Make sure you're choosing the History brush and not the Art History brush – there's a big difference!)

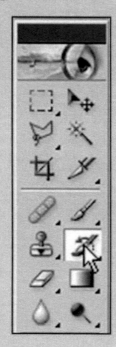

In the History palette, choose the original image as the return state by clicking on the box beside it as shown below.

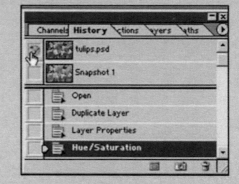

6. Now choose a brush you like and set the diameter so that you can start filling in the main flower. I loaded the default brushes, choosing a hard round brush set at 100px. To start, I've also set the opacity to 100%.

7. Start painting the main flower, slowly restoring the color to its petals and taking care to avoid the edge of the petal tips. When you've filled in the bulk of the color, switch to a smaller brush to paint the tips of the flower. Be careful not to paint outside of the petals, as this is the only one we want at 110% opacity.

8. At this point if you are happy with the image, take another snapshot using the camera icon at the bottom of the History Panel.

9. Now let's add some of the color to the background flowers. For this choose a spatter brush set at around 100px. Turn the Opacity down to around 50% and turn the airbrush option on. Start filling in the flowers, using the airbrush option to give darker and lighter effects. Take some snapshots along the way, so you can easily revert back if need be.

6

10. Finally turn the Opacity of the brush down even more to around 35% and pass over the two top corners of the image to show the blue in the sky slightly. By giving the sky some color we are adding a splash of contact to an otherwise pink image. Also it helps to balance the image aesthetically.

The same techniques work well on other floral shots too:

 From here you can take the image further using various filters. Check out Chapter 8 – Creating Works of Art to learn about filters.

6

6

6

Chapter 7
Magazine Retouching Techniques

Whether you're a professional photographer or not, you will probably have more than a suspicion that the pictures we see in magazines are not printed without a substantial amount of tweaking and touching up. Virtually every photo in fashion and beauty magazines has been visited by the Photoshop fairy. It's reassuring to know that it is actually impossible to look that perfect naturally – but if you want to give yourself or your subjects a quick Photoshop facial, or maybe even some digital plastic surgery, this chapter's the one for you!

In this chapter, we are going to use Photoshop 7's new **Healing Brush** tool to erase blemishes and facial lines, in combination with the **Clone Stamp** tool to even out skin tones. We'll also make use of the **Transform** function to make our model a little more plastic-perfect.

A common problem, especially with digital photography, is that the pictures you get seem to lack perspective, meaning that the subject and the background seem to merge into one. We'll be looking at how to create a shallower depth of field, to make our subject "jump off the page" and grab our attention. With this in mind, we will also add **catch-lights** (reflections from the light source) to our model's eyes, to bring them to life.

We'll also use the transformation options and Clone tools to make our subject appear taller and thinner in a high key fashion image.

Close up

- Healing Brush tool
- Clone Stamp tool
- Transform tool
- Brush tool
- Blur

1. Open up the image titled `Model1.tif`, located in the Chapter 7 folder.

> *If you are using your own images, bear in mind that you should have already color corrected your photo and adjusted the contrast before you start.*

2. Let's start by creating a duplicate layer and hiding our background layer. I've named this layer *Base*.

> *When doing any major changes in Photoshop, it's always good practice to make a duplicate layer to work from in case you don't like the end result. The history panel is great for going back a few steps, but you can only go so far back with it.*

Take a moment and examine the image.

> *When retouching any image first take a good look at it and make some notes as to what you want to do. This way you can prioritize what should be tackled first.*

The model herself is attractive, but her complexion is far from what you'd see in Vogue. Her lips are a bit thin and she has some bags under her slightly bloodshot eyes. Yikes!

We are going to use Photoshop 7's new Healing tool for the cheeks and forehead of our model and then use the Rubberstamp Tool to remove the model's nose piercing. From there we will start on the dark circles and lines under her eyes, the finally move on to plumping up the lips.

Blitzing those zits

For this image we are going to start first by getting rid of imperfections in the model's complexion. Enlarge the image to a size that's comfortable for you to work with.

With the Base layer active, select the Healing Brush tool.

The Healing Brush tool works much like the Clone Stamp tool in that we sample a part of the image to use by pressing the ALT/OPT key while clicking the mouse. Unlike the Clone Stamp tool, the Healing Brush tool blends our sampled area with the texture and tone of the area we want to retouch. This is what makes it terrific for facial complexions.

2. Let's take a moment to set our brushes to around Diameter 191px, Hardness 12%, Spacing 16%, Angle 0°, Roundness 100% and Size "off". Leave the blending mode at Normal and the Aligned option unchecked.

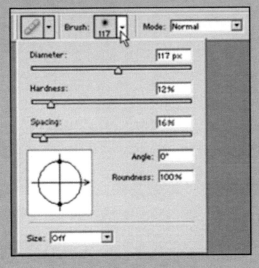

3. Starting on the forehead we will work our way around the model's face blending and removing any imperfections. Begin by sampling an area to use as our "retouch source" by using the ALT/OPT key mentioned above. Now move the tool over a blemished area on the forehead. Notice how the Healing Brush tool blends the texture and luminosity of the image.

 Don't worry if the area appears darker when you first apply the brush – it blends when you release the mouse.

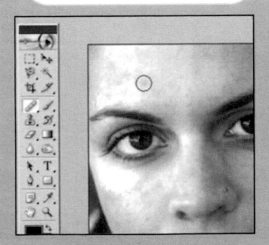

4. Lets do this again for the other areas adjusting our brush size to Diameter 100px. Now start removing the four beauty marks from the model's face – re-sampling and adjusting the brush size as you need to.

Now let's get rid of the nose piercing. If you try healing this area with the techniques we just applied the contrast between the blue of the nose ring and the model's skin is too much. The Healing Brush tool tries to blend the two leaving traces of blue. Rather than going over it several times to remove it, we are going to instead switch over to the Clone Stamp tool.

If you have tried using the Healing Brush tool for this in your image, go back the necessary steps in the History Palette.

7

5. Magnify the image so that you can comfortably work on the piercing and select the Clone Stamp tool.

159

6. Choose a brush size of around 45px with a feathered edge. Leave the blending mode at Normal, the Opacity and Flow at 100% and make sure the Aligned option is checked.

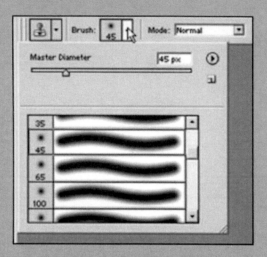

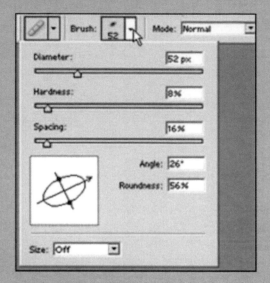

7. Work around the piercing, sampling new areas as we go, to remove all traces of the nose ring as illustrated below.

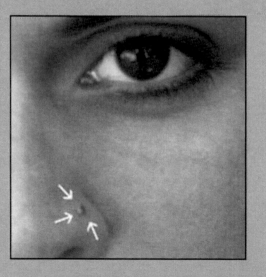

8. Now switch back to the Healing Brush tool so we can remove some of the fine lines and other imperfections on our model's face. Start on the left eye. Set the brush to: Diameter 52px, Hardness 8%, Spacing 16%, Angle 26° and Roundness 56%.

9. Sample an area near the eyes and apply the Healing Brush tool along the lowest line under the eye. If you are happy with the result, move to the next line. If not, undo, re-sample and re-apply.

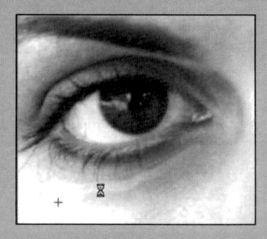

10. For the next line, adjust your Brush size, Angle and Roundness to begin removing the next facial line, taking care not to erase the lower lashes. Then do the right eye.

11. Apply the same techniques to any other imperfections in the skin and to the lines around the model's mouth on the left using the Healing Brush tool. I've chosen to keep the line on the right of the face as it keeps the image looking natural.

7

Take a look at how it looks so far. Not bad!

Transform

Now let's plump up her lips a little using the Transform options. The Transform options/submenu, according to Adobe, "lets you apply specific transformations to a selection, layer, path, vector shape, or selection border." Descriptive, eh? What this means is that we can select the whole image, or any part, and change it's shape as we see fit. Fantastic, but of course we have to be careful to mak it look real. Big changes are right out.

1. Before we move forward, take a snapshot of this state by clicking on the snapshot icon in the History palette. By taking a snapshot we are temporarily preserving this state so we can easily return to it if we don't like what we've done.

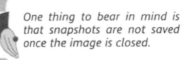

One thing to bear in mind is that snapshots are not saved once the image is closed.

2. We are going to fatten up the upper lip to give her a pout, which is very popular in magazines. To do this, select the upper portion of the lips using the Polygonal Lasso tool.

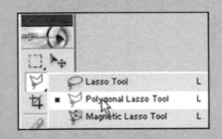

3. Make sure the Feather is set to 1px here and carefully select the upper lip. Magnify the image as large as you need to, to do this accurately as possible.

4. Choose the Free Transform option under **Edit > Free Transform** or CTRL/⌘-T on the keyboard.

5. Using the bounding box that now surrounds the upper lip, drag from the top right corner to increase the size of the lip, or enter in the width at 120 and height at 145 in their respective boxes in the options palette on the top of the screen.

7

6. As you are doing this, you may have noticed that the lips themselves are repositioned in the models face, slightly off from their original place. Once you have increased the size, click inside the transform box and drag the lips back to where they should be and press either the check mark on the Tool options bar or ENTER on the keyboard to accept the transformation.

11. Deselect all by pressing CTRL/⌘-D on the keyboard.

Take a look at the image so far.

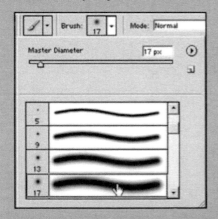

7. Deselect all by pressing CTRL/CMD-D on the keyboard and take a look. The upper lips looks fuller, but the angle is off – she's looking a little freaky rather than glamorous. We will remedy this by adjusting the perspective of the lips. In the History Palette, go back one step to restore the selection on the lips, or go to **Edit > Undo,** or press CTRL/⌘-Z.

8. With the lips still selected choose **Edit > Transform > Perspective**.

Brightening the whites of her eyes
We need to remove the red in her eyes. Have you ever seen a model in a magazine with bloodshot eyes? I haven't either.

9. This time we are going to use the bounding box lines between the points to adjust the image. This will change the horizontal skew of the lip so we can match the bottom lip. Grab the top line and slowly drag it to the left until the skew is matching the bottom lip.

1. Start by magnifying the eyes so you can comfortably work with them. We are going to use the Brush tool to literally paint over the red parts of the eyes. Select the Brush tool and select a Soft Round Brush around 17px (located in your default brushes). Set the Opacity to around 30%.

10. Next we are going to change the rotation of the lip. Grab the top right corner of the box and slowly drag it upwards to create a slight rotation. As you do this the size of the image will change as well. Play with this until you get an effect you like or just punch in the settings below to match what we used here.

2. Use the Eyedropper tool to sample a clear portion of the left eye to use as the paint. As you select the color it replaces the current foreground color. (By using a color already present the painting we are going to do will look more natural than choosing a color from the swatches.)

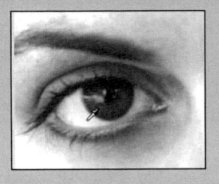

Final skin tone changes

An optional additional effect is to give the whole image a slightly soft focus look, which makes the skin tone appear just that bit more smooth.

1. Duplicate the image layer we've been working on (dragging the layer and dropping it on the new layer icon at the bottom of the Layers palette).

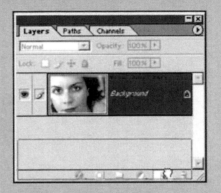

3. Now begin painting the white of the left eye, taking care not to paint over any of the iris or lids. If you need to, decrease the size of the brush as you get to the corners of the eye. When you have finished it, zoom out to take a look at it.

2. Apply a **Filter > Blur > Gaussian Blur** to the new layer, with a radius of about 3 px.

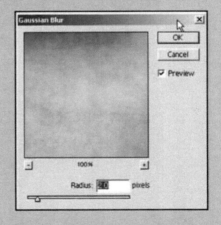

4. If you like what you see, move on to the right eye. Use the same color that we already sampled from the left eye, but lower the Opacity down to around 15%. Again change brush sizes as you need to, to cover the entire area.

3. Reduce the opacity of the new layer to approximately 60%, or whatever suits.

7

Your final image now has a soft focus effect – a higher blur factor makes it more dramatic.

You can sharpen certain areas by applying a mask to the blurred layer, as in the final example of this chapter.

7

Creating Catchlights

- Dodge tool
- Brushes

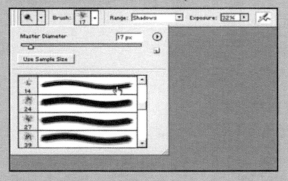

Now we are going to add **catchlights** in the eyes of the model in the image below. 'Catchlights' is the term used to describe the reflection of an image's light source in the subject's eyes (such as a flash). They add interest and life to eyes. In the case of this image, there was no direct light used to create the effect so we're going to add them.

1. Open up `catchlights.tif` in the Chapter 7 images folder.

2. Make a duplicate of the background layer and name it Catchlights. Hide the background layer and work off the Catchlights layer.

   Take a look at the image. What size should the catchlights be? What shape? The answers to these questions will depend on the image you are using. For this image we are going to create long narrow catchlights along the top of the iris and smaller ones in the bottom mimicking the angle of the highlights on the model's cheeks. (I chose

to create narrow rectangular catchlights to keep in tune with the shapes already in the image. If you look at the image, most of the shapes are rectangular.)

3. Magnify the image so you can work comfortably on the eyes. With the Catchlights layer active, select the Dodge tool.

4. Select a Spatter brush from the Brush menu and adjust the pixel size to around 17px. Have the Range set to Shadows, the Exposure set to around 32% and enable the Airbrush option.

Using a Spatter brush will give a random pattern for our catchlights, helping them to look like a natural reflection. The Airbrush option allows us to control how much light the brush "adds". The longer you hold down the mouse, the more of a dodge there will be.

7

5. Start with the left eye. We are going to create a catchlight in the top of the iris along the left as pointed out below.

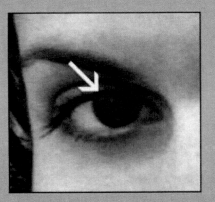

6. Start dodging the area where the catchlight will be. Vary how long you hold down the mouse to mimic various contrasts. If you think it's too light, or don't like the shape, use the History palette to take as many steps back as you need.

The idea here is to create a natural looking "highlight" in the eye. Between dodges, zoom out to view the effect in relation to the entire image.

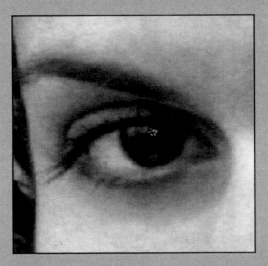

7. Once you are happy with your "highlight", start on the bottom right of the same eye to finish the effect.

8. Move to the right eye and repeat the effect. However this time make the top "highlight" slightly smaller and the bottom one larger.

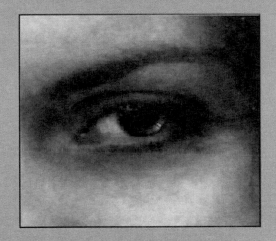

Great! Let's take a look at the finished product. Subtle, yet effective!

7

Depth of field

- Lasso tool
- Alpha channels
- Noise filter
- Blending modes

Taking the previous image, we can also add to the drama by creating a shallower depth of field.

1. Open up image great_depth.tif in the Chapter 7 folder. This is the complete image from the last task. (If you are working directly off the previous image, you must remove the background layer and rename the Catchlights layer Background before moving on.)

5. Turn on the visibility of the channel by clicking on the eye icon beside the Channel layer and deselect all using CTRL/⌘-D.

7

2. Duplicate the background layer and name it Blur. Hide the background layer and activate the Blur layer.

3. We will start first by selecting the part we want to keep in focus – our model – by using the Polygonal Lasso tool. Leave the Lasso settings at their defaults.

4. Save the selection as an Alpha Channel by right/CTRL-clicking on the selection and choosing Save selection or by clicking on the Save selection as a channel button at the bottom of the Channels palette as illustrated . Name it Alpha1.

In photographs with shallow depth of field, there is always a plane of focus on each side of the subject that is also sharp. To make the image look natural we have to create a mask for this focus plane. In this image we only have the vertical focus plane to add – the fence plank that the model is leaning on.

6. Do this by selecting the Eraser tool and choosing a brush with soft edges. We're perfectly safe with a huge 200px eraser here.

7. In the Alpha1 channel we just created, start erasing the mask on the areas we are including in our focal plane.

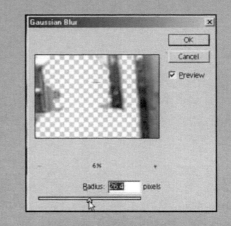

8. CTRL/⌘-click on the Alpha1 Channel to load it as a selection.

9. Return to the Layers palette and activate the Blur layer. We are going to move the subject that we are keeping in focus to a new layer by choose **Layer > New > Layer Via Cut**. Label it Model.

    Now we have three layers. The Background layer, the Blur layer and the Model layer. The reason we separated the area we want to blur from our model is to prevent the colors from bleeding where we don't want them.

Don't worry about the resulting gap between the cutout and the Blur layer. The original layer will fill that in. The next step is to hide any hints to what we've done, as when the Gaussian Blur erased the detail it also removed the film grain. The grainer the original image the more obvious this will be.

11. Activate the Blur layer. ALT/OPT-click on the Create New Layer icon on the bottom of the Layers palette. Name the layer Grain. In the same dialogue box, change the blending mode to Overlay and the select the Fill to Overlay-neutral color (50% gray) checkbox.

10. Activate the Blur layer. Go to **Filter > Blur > Gaussian Blur**. With the preview option on, adjust the blur to the effect you want. We used a 26.4 pixel radius here.

7

12. With the Grain layer chosen, select **Filter > Noise > Add Noise**. Play with the settings to achieve the effect you like. For this image I've chosen Monochromatic Noise with distribution of Gaussian set to an amount of 6.86%.

13. Activate the Blur layer. Change the blending mode in the Layers palette to Luminosity and the opacity to 88%.

14. The last step is to flatten our image. Turn the visibility of the Background layer on before choosing Flatten Image from the fly out panel in the Layers palette.

7

7

High keying

- Canvas Size
- Scale
- Clone Stamp tool
- Healing Brush tool
- Magnetic Lasso tool
- Motion Blur filter
- Film Grain filter

Now we are going to create a high-key fashion image using some of Photoshop's filters, and stretch our image to make the subject appear taller and thinner. A high-key image is one that uses a bright or white background, combined with light foreground colors. Conversely, an image with a dark or black background combined with dark colors in the foreground is called a low-key image.

1. Start by opening `girl.tif`. Duplicate the background layer and rename it Girl. Turn the visibility of the background layer off.

    Since the color and density has already been corrected we can go directly to the manipulation.

2. We are going to add some drama by stretching the image vertically. In order to do this we will first need to increase the height of our canvas to allow for this. Choose **Image > Canvas Size**. Change the height to 7 inches and click OK.

3. Now that we have some room to work let's make our subject look taller. Choose **Edit > Transform > Scale**. You are now presented with the bounding box around the entire image. Grab the handle in the middle of the top line and drag it up until you reach the top of the canvas. Then grab the handle on the bottom of the box and drag it until you reach the bottom of the box.

7

173

4. In the Scale options bar, at the top of your screen, your height should read at or around 126.8 %. Now change the width to 90 % by entering the value into the box. Press enter to accept the changes or press the checkmark on the options bar.

Take a look at what it has done to the image.

Now we're on the right track. The subject looks taller and thinner. Although we've stretched her a bit, she's not quite unreal, but it's certainly a more dramatic pose than a family photo.

5. Now we are going to manipulate the image again by removing the excess around her waist so she appears model thin. To do this select the Clone Stamp tool and choose a hard edged brush set to around 19px. Make sure the Opacity is at 100%.

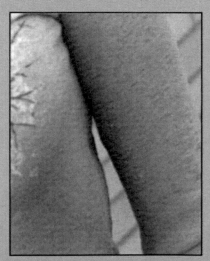

6. Look at the subject's waist and make note of how far in we are going to remove. You only want to go in so far as to create a straight line down her side.

We are using the Clone Stamp here instead of the Healing Brush as we want to completely remove the area. The Healing Brush tool would blend the two textures and densities together, which in this case is not the effect we want.

7. Begin by sampling a portion of the background by using the ALT/OPT key and start to shave down her waist.

8. Once you have shaved off the area and are happy with the result, select the Blur tool. Choose a soft edge brush at around 30px and set the Strength at 100%. Glide the brush over the edge we just shaved in order to minimize any "cut-out" effect. This will help to make the change we made appear more natural.

Your image should be similar to the one below.

Now we are going to use the Healing Brush tool to remove the folds in the fabric on the subject's arm, and on the top right of her shirt. In magazine and fashion photography, every movement and placement of a product is done with purpose. A fold in the fabric is not aesthetically pleasing and we want the "product" to look as appealing as possible.

7

Now we are ready to modify the background and transform the image into a high-key masterpiece.

11. Select the Magnetic Lasso tool. Set the Feather to 0px. Select the subject. Once you have done this, invert the selection by choosing **Select > Inverse** or by pressing CTRL/⌘-SHIFT-I on the keyboard. Now our background should be the selection.

9. Select the Healing Brush tool and choose a hard edged brush set to around 19px. Make sure the Opacity is set to 100%. I've chosen to start on her arm, as it's the simplest to fix. Sample an area and start going over the fabric folds until they disappear. Once you have completed this action, move to the top of the shirt and do the same with the folds on the chest area. Don't worry about the folds that are bulging on the edges, we'll take care of them later. If necessary, toggle between brush sizes to make sure that the pattern in the shirt remains unaffected.

10. Once you are done, switch back to the Clone Stamp tool. Now we are going to remove the bulges on the edges of the sleeve. Choose a hard edge brush set to around 19px with the Opacity set to 100%, and begin to remove the bulges in the fabric in the same manner we shaved the subject's waist.

12. The first thing we want to do is eliminate the brick pattern, as it is distracting from our product. Go to **Filter > Blur > Motion Blur** and move the image in the preview window so that you can see the background. This way you can see the effect. Set the Distance to 251 and the Angle to -58 to match the angle of the subject.

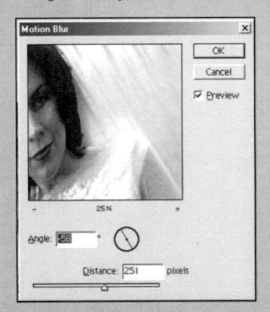

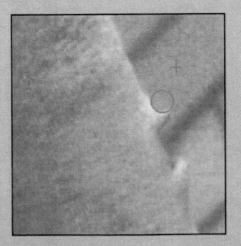

7

That's looking better, but our image is still not high-key. We will fix this by adding some film grain and manipulating the highlights and intensity features.

13. Go to **Filter > Artistic > Film Grain**. Set the Grain to 4, the Highlight Area to 20 and the Intensity to 7.

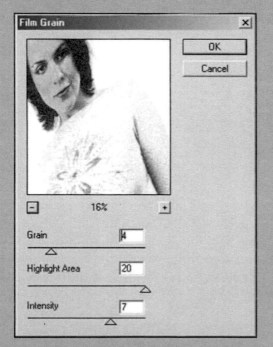

Job done. Now she'd look perfectly at home on the front of a home shopping catalogue.

7

Folds and ripples

- Layer via Copy
- Polygonal Lasso tool
- Free Transform tool
- Healing Brush tool
- Clone Stamp tool
- Linked Layers
- Layer Opacity

In this image, we want to prepare our model to appear on the page, which in this case means tidying up any problems with her clothing and the original digital source. As with any project, it always helps to identify the 'flaws', such as they are, with the image. Remember, it's a good idea to discuss this sort of thing with the client – their view of the perfect image may well differ from yours.

On this image we should consider the following corrections:

- Her shirt has folded a little unfortunately just above her belt, so it'd be nice to iron this out for her.
- There are a couple of creases on the back of her left leg.
- The angle of the camera gives a dramatic pose, but it makes her face seem a little square-on in comparison to her body. We need to compensate for this somehow.
- It would also be nice to tone her lips and smooth out her skin to give that magazine sheen.
- Make an allowance for the digital source.

So, without further ado:

1. The first thing to do, once the image is open, is to duplicate our background layer and save as a PSD (Photoshop) file. As always, it is safer to work on the assumption that the client might change their minds on certain aspects, so we need to try to use 'non-destructive editing' – work that can be amended easily.

2. That safely accomplished, let's deal with the last of our observations first – the digital source. A quick Sharpen filter might be the simplest solution, as there doesn't seem to be much of a colorcast. **Filter > Sharpen**.

7

Tailor made

It's probably best to start with the more 'structural' changes – those involving changes to the apparent shape – and to leave the 'touching up' (skin tone for example) until afterwards. With that in mind let's zoom in on that unsightly fold identified above.

1. Select a region around the fold to be removed, with a feather of a few pixels – the exact amount should depend on the resolution of your image, but here I used 3px.

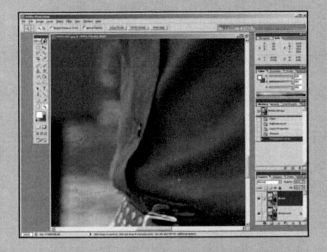

2. Click CTRL/⌘-J to create a new layer via copy. Give it a sensible name like 'tummy' so you know what your new layer is going to affect.

3. Reselect your area on your new layer (if Photoshop won't let you, use the Magic Wand to select the invisible area outside, then invert your selection). Press CTRL/⌘-T to apply the Free Transform tool to the region.

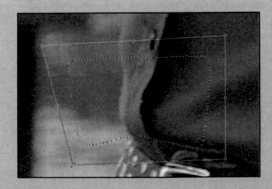

4. Holding CTRL/⌘ as you click on the corner points, distort the image so that the line of the shirt seems better. Don't worry about anything except the edge in front of the canal – the rest we'll get to in a minute. Once you've moved the bottom left corner, you may need to move the top left one the other way so that the fold still lines up.

5. When you're happy with the changes click the tick in the Tool Options bar. You can check your result by turning the layer visibility on and off in the Layers palette.

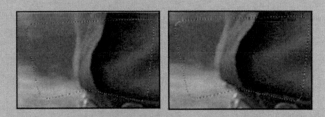

6. Now select the Clone Stamp tool, and uncheck the 'Aligned' and check the 'Use All Layers' boxes in the Tool Options bar. By aligning our stamp, we start from the same source point each time we click – handy for following straight lines.

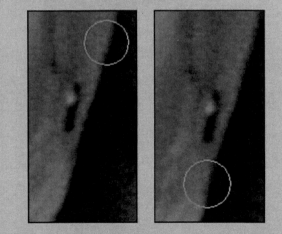

7. Select an undamaged area of the line and apply it, using a soft edged brush, lower down where the join of our transformation is evident.

8. Continue with the Clone Stamp tool to straighten out the whole region. It may help to switch the 'Aligned' feature on once you've got a rough line that you are happy with.

7

9. If necessary, use the Healing Brush tool to re-apply some texture over the area, then zoom out to admire your handiwork.

10. All we need to do now, using a lower opacity Clone Stamp, is to tone-down the effect of the creases that point in the direction of the fold we removed.

11. Create a new blank layer, and name it 'Jeans', or whatever suits.

12. Uncheck the 'Aligned' function of the Clone Stamp again, and select an area where the angle of her leg matches the area you are going to replace and get rid of those creases.

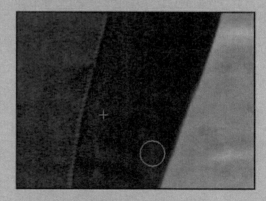

13. Again, the Healing Brush tool is useful for restoring the texture that you lose if you use a softer, low opacity Clone Stamp.

We can now apply the same technique we used to tidy up our transformation on the creases in our model's jeans, using the Clone Stamp.

Best angle

Perhaps the most risky part of our plan is to try and move the model's face to a more flattering angle. This is definitely a time where we should allow subtlety to act as our guiding hand, rather than getting carried away.

1. As with the shirt, select the model's face using the Elliptical Lasso tool with a feather of a couple of pixels. We can see immediately where the problem areas are going to crop up.

2. Ensuring that you have the model layer selected, use CTRL/⌘-J to create a new layer via copy, and name the layer accordingly.

3. As before, use the Free Transform facility, and this time drag the face in slightly from the left hand side to narrow it. This clearly isn't the perfect solution but it is a lot easier than re-taking the photo.

It is also possible to apply the Liquify tool to the layer to make any minor adjustments to a face using the same layers technique – this might be more appropriate for other similar cases..

4. Using the Clone Stamp and judiciously switching the 'Aligned' option on and off, it is a fairly simple process to repair the hair at the top left of our transformation. At the bottom there is the more complex matter of dealing with the shirt collar.

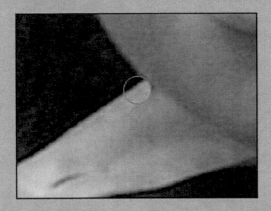

5. We can start by reconstructing the line of the collar with a hard-edged Clone Stamp at 100% opacity. We then need to subtly restore the shadow, which has been affected by our feathering. This is easier with a soft edged brush of a smaller size. Remember to check under the chin as well.

6. As a final touch, a very low opacity burn tool might get the shadow just right.

Check for any other abnormalities.

Adding that magazine sheen

If you can't think of anything else that needs changing, we'll round off by giving her a magazine style 'gloss finish'. It is probably wise to create a copy of our 'Face' layer at this point and work on that.

1. Select the Dodge tool (under the Burn tool) set the Range to Highlights and choose a low Exposure setting, then brush gently over the whites of our models eyes to lighten them a little.

2. Moving on to the mouth, select the Sponge tool, set the mode to desaturate and use it to gently brush our model's teeth.

3. We could also try the Sponge tool, set on saturate, to bring the lips out a bit. First select them using the Lasso or Polygonal Lasso (feathered slightly) and then put them on a different layer, giving us more flexibility. CTRL/⌘-J after selecting them.

4. Create a Hue/Saturation adjustment layer with a slight move towards the red hue. Then link this layer with the layer below it.

5. Now click **Layer > Group Linked** (CTRL/⌘-G). This will basically mean that you can adjust the lipstick as and when you feel like it by double clicking on the grouped adjustment later. Make any final adjustments now you can see the contrast with the background.

7

6. Back to our Face Copy layer, let's apply that final sheen. Select the Healing Brush tool and select an area somewhere on the cheek, then draw a line under each eye. Once you let go, any hint of a lack of sleep will disappear.

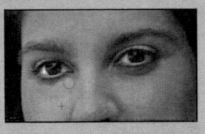

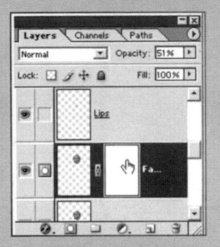

7. Apply this technique to any other small blemishes on the face. Here these are few and far between, but were aiming at a glossy effect.

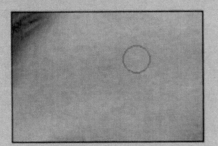

8. Now duplicate our face copy layer one more time. Apply a Gaussian blur to the new layer of about 3 pixels, more or less depending on the effect you're going for.

9. Reduce the opacity of that new layer, which should be just above the Face layer, to about 50% – whatever you think looks best.

10. As this effectively reduces some details we want to keep, select **Layer > Add Layer Mask > Reveal All**.

11. Ensuring that your new layer mask is selected, choose a soft edged brush and paint over areas where you'd like to retain detail. These are probably the eyes, nostrils and eyebrows (the lips retain detail as their layer is above anyway).

12. It might balance things a little to go over the neck area with the Blur tool to mimic the facial effect slightly (you can always recover by erasing the Blurred area and revealing the original underneath.

7

And that, as they say, is that. Here is a layer breakdown and the final image. By turning off layer visibility, we can turn our various changes on and off to suit the client (assuming we save as a Photoshop PSD, that is).

Chapter 8
Creating Works of Art

Artistic composition is defined as the way parts of an image are arranged. It is not only a way of clarifying images, but of recognizing visual problems. If composition was the furthest thing from your mind when you took your picture, then consider Photoshop as the closest thing to a re-write! The elements of composition – line, shape, tone, and texture – are the building blocks of every image.

Line is the fundamental element of composition. Lines make the edges of shapes, provide clues for motion (or lack of it), and suggest subtle conceptual meanings. They draw your eye over the image in a certain direction, controlling how you perceive the information contained within it.

Vertical lines are used to depict power, strength, rigidity, and height. Horizontal lines give a suggestion of calmness, passivity, breadth, weight, finality, and distance. Angled lines suggest motion and strong action, whereas curved lines are associated with grace, beauty, love, and nature. Finally, jagged lines indicate tension, anger, confusion, and chaos, as your eye is drawn in many different directions, resulting in conflict within the visual experience. It's the specific combination of these lines that make or break an image visually. It is these lines that create works of art.

By leaving these 'lines', the core of any image, intact, we can create any number of different feels or effects. Color, form, and texture all play a pivotal role in the success of your work. And luckily for us, Photoshop makes playing with these factors easy – we don't have to spend hours in the darkroom to achieve these effects. Let's have a look at how you can use texture to transform your photographs.

Creating a texture sandwich

- Drag and drop
- Layers
- Render filter

Art really is in the eye of the beholder and what often separates "straight" photography from art – art that people are willing to pay big bucks for – is texture. Sandwiching negatives has been a technique employed by photographers to turn their images into works of art. The trick is to combine an image of a colorful, evenly lit subject with another image that is light colored or over-exposed, or a textured background. In Photoshop, traditional sandwiching is easily accomplished through the use of layers and layer opacity.

1. Create a new 6x4in file. Set the Resolution to 300ppi and the Mode to RGB Color.

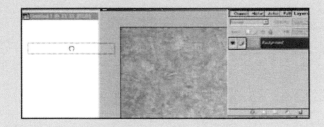

2. Now open texture.tif.

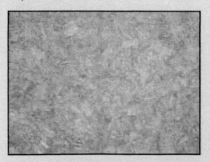

3. Copy this image onto the new canvas by dragging the 'Background' layer on to the blank canvas we just created. The image is automatically placed on a new layer. Rename the layer 'texture'. Use the Move tool to re-position the image on the canvas.

4. Now open model.tif.

5. Copy this image over to our blank canvas as well. Rename the layer 'model'.

6. Use the Move tool to center the image on the canvas. Move the 'texture' layer above the 'model' layer. Adjust the opacity of the 'texture' layer to around 40%.

8

Voila! A texture sandwich! It's just that easy.

Taking the sandwiching technique further

We are going to take it a step further by slightly softening and adding some depth to the 'texture' layer – something that cannot be done with traditional sandwiching techniques.

1. Activate the 'texture' layer. Make sure that your foreground and background colors are set to their defaults by pressing the letter D on the keyboard.

    Choose **Filter > Render > Difference Clouds**. Adjust the layer opacity to around 31%.

With Photoshop you can take this darkroom technique a few steps further by sandwiching as many images as you like – taken at any exposure.

2. Open granite.tif and drag it over to our working canvas.

Reposition it on the canvas using the Move tool and rename the layer 'granite'.

3. Adjust the layer opacity to 34%. The granite texture has helped soften our original texture.

4. Now select the 'model' layer. Our texture layers have muted our subject a little too much. Choose **Image > Adjustments > Brightness/Contrast**. Set the Brightness to –9 and the Contrast to +13.

That's looking better! And here's our final image.

8

189

Rough pastels with filters

- Magnetic Lasso tool
- Artistic filters
- Render filters
- Brush stroke filters

Photoshop's **Filter** menu easily mimics "texture sandwiches" with a variety of textures, brushes, strokes, and much more. You can simulate old media styles, such as oil painting, using filters on your photos. A word of warning though – all too often filters are used in a way that allows you to immediately spot them. Subtlety is the key here.

1. Open tulip.tif.

Duplicate the 'Background' layer and rename it 'tulip'. Hide the 'Background' layer and activate the 'tulip' layer.

2. Select the Magnetic Lasso tool.

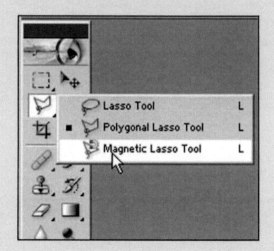

Make sure the settings are as follows:

- Feather: 0px
- Anti-Aliased: checked
- Width: 10px
- Edge contrast: 10%
- Frequency: 57

3. Using the Lasso, select the two main tulips in the foreground. If you need to, swap to the Polygonal Lasso tool and use the **add** or **subtract** selection options on the tool menu to add or erase parts of the image.

8

4. Invert the selection by either choosing **Select > Inverse** or using the shortcut CTRL/⌘-SHIFT-I.

5. Move our selection to a new layer by choosing **Layer > New > Layer Via Cut**. Rename this layer 'canvas'.

6. With the new layer selected take a moment to make sure that your foreground and background

colors are set to their defaults by pressing the letter D on the keyboard. Now choose **Filter > Artistic > Underpainting**. Use the settings as shown below, and click OK.

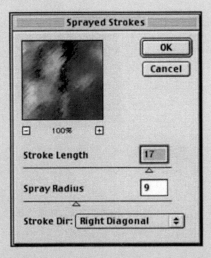

7. Now choose **Filter > Brush Strokes > Sprayed Strokes**, using the settings shown here, and click OK.

8. Merge the 'tulip' layer and the 'canvas' layer by selecting **Merge Visible** from the layers palette context menu.

8

191

Let's add a lighting effect to this image to add interest to the sky.

9.   Go to **Filter > Render > Lens Flare**. Adjust the settings as shown below, and place the flare at the top of the image, towards the right, to fit in with the flow and existing light patterns of the image. Click OK.

Rough Pastels

OK
Cancel

100%

Stroke Length   4

Stroke Detail   1

Texture: Canvas

Scaling   100 %

Relief   20

Light Dir: Top

☐ Invert

By going through these different filters, the goal is to create texture in a non-uniform manner. Despite the fact that Photoshop has fantastic filters, they are sometimes applied too evenly. A piece of art that has been hand-painted, the effect we are trying to simulate, is not typically perfectly uniform. There are subtleties in color and texture that artists employ in their technique – consciously or subconsciously.

10.   Now go to **Filter > Artistic > Rough Pastels**. Set the options as shown here and press OK.

11.   We're also going to add a Drybrush effect to the image. Go to **Filter > Artistic > Dry Brush**. Use the settings shown and click OK.

8

Lens Flare   ✕

Brightness: 171 %   OK

                                                  Cancel

Flare Center:

Lens Type:
○ 50-300mm Zoom
● 35mm Prime
○ 105mm Prime

Dry Brush   ✕

                                                  OK
                                                  Cancel

50%

Brush Size   5

Brush Detail   10

Texture   1

Let's take a look at the finished product. It looks like a painting.

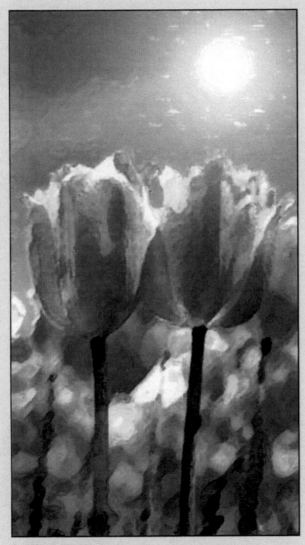

© *Photos by Nyree*

For this image, the Dry Brush filter was applied first, then the Rough Pastels filter.

One of the great things about using filters is how the final product varies depending on the order the filters are applied. Take a look at the examples below:

This image uses the Rough Pastel filter only.

8

Polaroid transfers

- Adjustment layers
- Eraser tool
- Filters

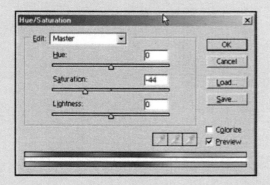

Polaroid transfers are the closest traditional photography gets to painting. This technique involves literally transferring an image from a developing sheet of Polaroid film on to something else – such as a textured piece of paper. During this transfer, the colors become pastel, the receiving paper picks up the bubbly edge of the developing fluids, and the texture of the paper comes through. We are going to create this effect using Photoshop, with one of the images from the previous example.

1. Open up tulip_pastels.psd, or you can use your own image.

2. Duplicate the 'Background' layer and name it 'pastel'. Now hide the 'Background' layer.

We have already simulated the texture of a canvas in the previous example, now we are going to mute the colors down and make them look like pastels.

3. Go to **Image > Adjust > Hue/Saturation**. Set the Saturation to around -44. Notice how the colors mute to give a soft pastel feel.

Your image should look like the image over the page.

8

Next we are going to simulate the uneven and bubbly edges that accompany a traditional transfer.

4. Choose the Eraser tool and select a spatter brush of 39px. Set the Opacity to 31%. Start erasing parts of the edges of the image at random, to give an uneven, patchy effect to the edges of the picture.

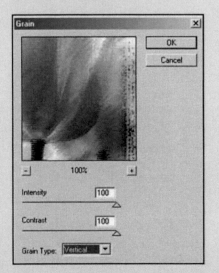

5. Choose the Rectangular Marquee tool and set the Feather to 8px. Draw a rectangle about a half-inch inside the image. Now choose **Select > Inverse** (CTRL/⌘-SHIFT+I) to select the inverse.

6. Go to **Filter > Texture > Grain**. Set the Intensity and Contrast to 100 and the Grain Type to Vertical. (Only the areas selected in the marquee will be affected so move the preview window to the edges to preview the effect.)

8

Click OK, and then deselect all (CTRL/⌘-D).

7. Still using the Rectangular Marquee, select the right side of the image. (Keep the feather at 8px.)

9. Deselect again and re-select a narrower slice on the right, this time leaving around a half-inch on the top and bottom.

8. Now go to **Filter > Noise > Add Noise**. Apply the settings as shown and click OK.

10. Go to **Filter > Sketch > Torn Edges**. Apply the settings as shown below.

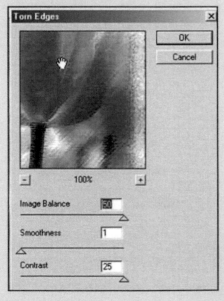

11. Deselect all, and select a slightly wider area on the right. Go to **Filter > Texture > Grain**. Apply the settings as shown below and click OK. Deselect all.

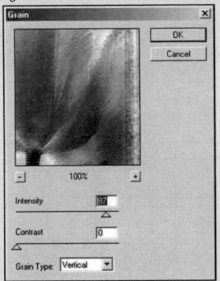

12. Again using the Rectangular Marquee, select the top edge. Go to **Filter > Brush Strokes > Ink Outlines**. Set the Stroke Length and Dark Intensity to 50 and the Light Intensity to 0, and click OK.

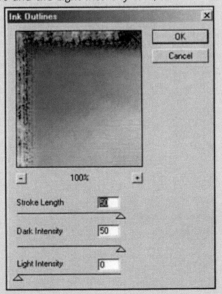

13. Select the bottom edge with the Rectangular Marquee tool. Go to **Filter > Artistic > Underpainting**. Apply the settings as shown:

We're almost there. For the final touch we are going to create developing fluid bubbles.

14. Using the Polygonal Lasso tool, select an irregular area at the top of the image.

8

15. Go to **Filter** > **Texture** > **Craquelure**. Set the Crack Spacing to 8, the Crack Depth to 3 and the Crack Brightness to 7.

16. Deselect all. Turn on the visibility of the 'Background' layer and merge the layers. Here we have an image whose edges looks somewhat like they would in a Polaroid transfer. Another method for doing this would be to scan a Polaroid transferred image and create a pattern of the edges to use in other works.

8

Denied: Digital Art by Vikas Shah

- Digital camera
- Crop
- Adjustment layers
- Extract filter
- Motion Blur

Denied is a piece from the "Living Colour" series by UK-based Vikas Shah, the image was originally a digital photograph taken in Manchester city center with a Nikon Coolpix 885 digital camera (with camera controlled aperture and shutter speed). The following takes you through the steps from pressing the shutter to digital art, though you could easily use the technique on your own pictures to add effects to individual parts of pictures.

As with any photograph, composition is crucial to gain visual equilibrium on the image. As well as looking at the general balance of the picture, as you would for any photograph, consideration must be given to any individual elements within the picture that will form the focus of the artwork. In other words, is there a clear subject?

It often helps to take a few different shots composing the scene slightly differently to give you a selection of shots to choose from. For the purposes of this technique, you need not be too fussy with aperture or shutter speed – the camera auto will usually suffice - so long as you capture the *detail* of the picture.

The photograph used for "Denied" was taken in an alleyway near Chinatown in central Manchester. The composition was intended to give a very "urban" feel to the photograph, showing the grit of the city center together with the key element of the yellow lines on the road (*very prominent on the photo and the influence for the name*).

We will take you through how the photograph was converted from being merely a picture of an alleyway to the final "Denied" digital art piece, in part black & white and part color. At each stage, ensure you **always** remember your chosen element or subject. You must ensure that if

you apply any effects or changes to your photograph, that your subject/element is always kept in the best possible character.

1. You need to trim the image to match your target output. In this case, the original image was resized to be roughly in proportion to A4 (*210mm x 190mm*). A portion of the image roughly in proportion was selected carefully. If in doubt, always make it slightly "over" selected so that you can crop to exact size later. Care was taken to ensure that no "unnatural" cuts were made (*for example: cutting off the edge of a box on the road or through a key element*). Once selected, simply go to Image->Crop to remove the unwanted parts of the image. You should then be left with a nicely proportioned image to begin working with (a)

8

2. The next step is to resize your image to your target size. Its important to do this step now so that any changes you make later (particularly the artistic effects) are done at the correct resolution to avoid any distortion. The target output for this image was A4 (210mm x 290mm). To allow for page bleed, the actual output size of the picture would need to be around 5mm larger than your target (depending on your printer). So for our piece, the output would be W215mm x H295mm.

In Photoshop, go to **Image > Image Size**, and then ensure the proportions of the image are constrained (*click on Constrain Proportions*). Our target output resolution is 300dpi, so a resample is also needed (*ensure Resample Image is selected*). Bicubic is by far the best algorithm for resampling photographs, giving a nice even effect.

In our example, the resolution was entered as 300, and the image height changed to 29.5cm (*giving approximately 22/25cm width depending on your selection prowess*). Once resized, if your width was slightly too large, go to **Image > Canvas Size** and resize to the exact size.

If you are left with any jagged or unnatural edges on your photograph, you can apply the Blur tool from your toolbar with a brush (around 40-50% pressure) to get rid of them. Digital cameras are also known for their poor edge quality, you may also wish to therefore enhance the edges on your picture **Filter > Sharpen > Sharpen edges**.

3. If you zoom in to "actual size" on this image, you will now see, depending on the output resolution of your digital camera, the quality of the resample. As a guide, for digital photography, a 2Mpix camera will give little noticeable distortion at A4/300dpi but is unsuitable for anything larger.

4. As you can see, the colors in our original are somewhat washed, lacking in vividness. In Photoshop, go to **Image > Adjust > Brightness/Contrast**. Using the sliders, increase the Contrast in the picture until the colors are more vivid (*without losing too much detail*) and then adjust the Brightness until the image looks visually balanced. In our piece, the Contrast was taken to around 32 and the Brightness to around 15. Remember here also to ensure that when you raise the Contrast, you do not lose detail on your subject (*in our case, the yellow lines*).

5. Using the layers toolbar, create TWO duplicate layers of your picture and delete the 'Background' layer. To create the duplicates, right click on your image in the Layers palette (it will almost certainly be called 'Background') and click Duplicate layer. This first layer will be our black and white layer. Now follow the same procedure again and create another layer above this. This will be our color layer. The 'Background' layer is no longer particularly needed so you can select it and click the trash can icon to remove it. You should be left with two layers only.

8

You can also duplicate layers by dragging them onto the Create new layer button at the bottom of the Layers palette.

6. Make the top layer invisible, so you are only seeing the bottom one.

7. Select this bottom layer and create a Hue/Saturation adjustment layer for it, and using the "Master" channel, take the saturation right down to −100. This layer will now be in grayscale.

8. Now create a Brightness/Contrast adjustment layer, and adjust the sliders to gain some strong and balanced presence in the "environment" in which your element resides. In our example, even though some detail was lost, by giving greater contrast, the image was made to appear much stronger.

9. Make the top layer visible again and select it.

10. Go to **Filter > Extract** in your Photoshop tool bar (Extract is under the Image menu in Photoshop 6).

In your extract window, zoom in to approximately actual size on your picture and find the point where your element meets the edge of the page (*in our example, I initially took the viewer to the far bottom left of the screen*). You must now select your brush size and method.

11. If your element has quite defined edges against a complex background (*like on Denied*), use a fairly small brush (*I used a 5pixel one*). Smart highlighting will also help in this sense. Unless you are using a wider brush, you need not apply any smoothing. Now you must **carefully** select around your element, an art tablet is particularly useful for this, but otherwise, go slowly with a mouse. Keep the brush fairly central over the "edge" of your element (*in our case, the point where the line meets the road*) giving equal coverage on each side. Follow the natural lines of your element correcting even minor mistakes. In our piece, a number of separate elements were selected based on natural breaks in the lines on the road. Once complete, and still within the Extract window, simply use the Paint Bucket tool to fill your selections.

8

12. It is always wise to do a "preview" of your extraction to ensure you have been accurate and that there are no overly erroneous portions. Once you are happy, click "OK" and the final extraction will take place. You will then see your extracted element on your grayscale background.

13. In general, you will see that the element does look slightly out of place! The next step is to balance your element into its surroundings as well as making it a centerpiece in your artwork. To create the effect you see on Denied, a duplicate should be created of your extracted layer, giving three layers in total (not including adjustment layers).

14. Now remove visibility on the top layer.

15. On the middle layer (your original extraction), a slight motion blur can be added to balance the hard edges and give an interesting effect. Using **Filter > Blur > Motion Blur**, select an appropriate number of pixels (15 here).

    Now you can make the top layer visible again. Since we adjusted the Brightness/Contrast on the grayscale layer, the top layer looks slightly imbalanced.

16. A Brightness/Contrast adjustment layer can then be added to the top layer and the Contrast/Brightness adjusted to suit. On Denied the final adjustments were −5 brightness and +10 contrast.

    Any remaining jagged edges should now be corrected gently using the paintbrush and blur tool, with low (below 30%) pressure. This was the final stage in the production of Denied and of this example.

To illustrate this technique further, let's look at two more example pieces:

Ghost walker

City in church

The desired effect here was to create a slightly ethereal feel to the picture. The subject chosen was the individual walking and the picture was taken on the banks of the River Ganges, on an Olympus Mju II 35mm camera, using ISO200 film, and then scanned in at 600dpi on a standard flatbed. Using the same techniques described above, the final piece was created but with a much more marked motion blur as the **top** layer. You could also extract other elements of the image, like the trees, to change the tone.

This is a combination piece with the objective of creating "false reality". The idea is Escher-esque - to look real but be clearly impossible. The extraction technique was again used here but rather than using the same picture, elements were chosen from two separate images. One of the inside of a church in San Diego, CA and one of the San Francisco Skyline. The Brightness/Contrast and Color Saturation of each layer was then adjusted to ensure they appeared to match. Any jagged edges on the extracted skyline were then removed using a Blur tool. The finished picture gives the effect of a city inside a church!

8

8

Chapter 9
Infra-red Imaging and Cross-processing

Infra-red film and cross-processing are two things most photographers love to play with but are not used on a regular basis, as the results are hard to predict for all but the most skilled in the craft.

Infra-red films photograph the light that we see and the light that we don't see – infra-red light. Besides not being visible to the human eye, infra-red light cannot be read by any light meters. This makes obtaining a proper exposure a guessing game and much of the film is wasted on bracketing, which is essential.

Infra-red film gives a dreamlike quality to images. There is more infra-red light on bright sunny days than there is on cloudy days. For black and white infra-red film, clear skies turn dark, clouds stay white, reds go dark and greens go almost white. People's skin can glow with a soft light. Water can reflect infra-red if the surface is in motion, but absorbs it if it's still. Shallow water usually goes transparent, as more particles are visible to reflect infra-red light.

Color infra-red photography is often called *false color photography* because it renders the scene in different colors to those normally seen by the human eye. Greens appear in red tones. Very intense reds show healthy, dense vegetation, light reds and magentas indicate lower vigor and density. Soils (beiges and browns) are shown in shades of white, blue, or green – depending on the amount of moisture. Clear water turns black and darker waters show up in various shades of blue.

Cross-processing film has it's own unique quirks. A proper exposure can be obtained easily, but the color outcome depends on what type of film is used, in combination with the processing chemicals on any given day.

infra-red effects on black and white

- Magic Wand
- Feathering
- Render Filters

This section will cover how to create infra-red effects for both black & white and color images using a variety of filters and layer effects. It will also show how to create the color shifts and contrast that accompanies a cross-processed image – with controllable results.

1. Open `statue.tif` in the xxx folder and duplicate the 'Background' layer. Rename it 'sky' and hide the 'Background' layer.

2. Activate the 'sky' layer.

3. Select the Magic Wand tool. Set the Tolerance to 10, and make sure Anti-Aliased and Contiguous are checked. Select the areas of sky, as shown. Remember, hold Shift to add an area after your first.

4. With the sky selected we are going to set the feathering. Go to **Select > Feather**, and set it to 3.

Feathering softens the edges around a selection by making some of the pixels around it translucent. The number of pixels you choose should depend on the resolution of your image: 1 or 2 for a digital camera, more for a very high resolution image. 0.5 is the minimum setting.

5. Now we are going to darken the sky and add some interest. It's just so bland right now! As mentioned above, infra-red film typically darkens skies and leaves clouds fluffy, so a few clouds should add some interest to our image, creating a bit of a foreboding feel.

9

6. Go to **Filter > Render > Difference Clouds**.

7. Go to **Select > Inverse** or Ctrl/⌘-Shift-I in order to select the statue.

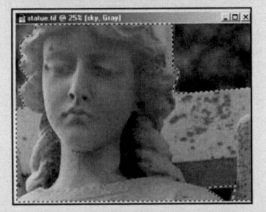

We are going to move the statue to a new layer. Separating the statue from the sky means that we can have different blending modes for each.

8. Choose **Layer > New > New Layer Via Cut** (Ctrl/⌘-Shift-J). Rename the layer 'statue'.

9. With the 'statue' layer activated, select **Filter > Distort > Diffuse Glow**. Apply the settings as shown.

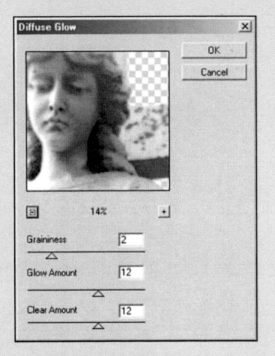

Turn on the visibility of the 'background' layer and select the 'sky' layer. Change the blending mode to Color Burn to create those fluffy clouds. Et voila!

9

infra-red on a color photo

- Invert
- Stylize Filters
- Replace Color
- Eyedropper
- Hue/Saturation

This time we will make a color image appear as though it was taken with color infra-red film.

1. Open `fence.tif`. Duplicate the background layer and rename it 'fence'. Hide the background layer.

pixel with its opposite brightness and/or color value.

2. Let's start by inverting the image. Go to **Image > Adjust > Invert** or CTRL/⌘-I. This inverts the image into a negative on the screen by replacing each

3. Now go to **Filter > Stylize > Diffuse**. Select **Darken Only**.

9

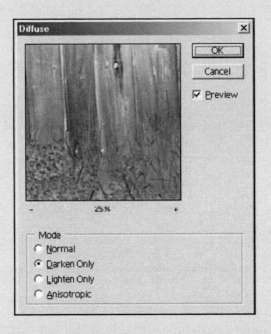

4. Let's punch up the colors more by going to **Image > Adjust > Equalize**. Equalizing an image redistributes the layer's brightness values and in the process improves overall contrast. Wow! What a difference!

We are now going to change the color of the grass to mimic the reds that would appear with color infra-red

photography.

5. Go to **Image > Adjustments > Replace Color**. Leave the option set to Selection and use the Eyedropper tool to sample the grass in our image.

Make sure the Eyedropper tool with the "+" is selected so that you can add to the selection, or alternatively hold down the SHIFT key. The selected areas will show up in the window as you go. If you select the wrong area, you can undo with CTRL/⌘-Z.

6. Once you have all of the grass area selected, use the Hue slider to select a red. (Mine is set to +85.) Set the Saturation to 100% and leave the Lightness at 0, and click OK.

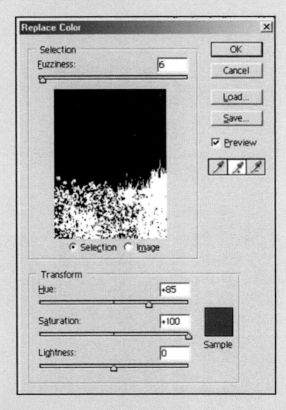

9

Your image should look similar to this one.

Now let's add some grain to the image to mimic the qualities of infra-red film.

7. Go to **Filter > Artistic > Film Grain**. Apply the settings as shown.

8. We are going to apply the Difference Clouds filter to the image. Before we do this, however, we better make sure we are working with the same colors. Your foreground should be a red and your background should be white.

> *You can set your foreground and background colors to the default settings by pressing the letter 'D' on your keyboard and invert them by pressing the letter "X" on the keyboard so white is now your background color.*

Change the foreground to a shade of red from the grass by using the Eyedropper tool. My shade of red is #FF170B.

Now go to **Filter > Render > Difference** Clouds. It makes our image look pretty good – actually, I quite like it, but it's not quite the infra-red effect we are going for. Keep in mind that your image may differ from mine as this filter varies in its application, which is one of the great things about it!

9. Invert the image by choosing **Image > Adjustments > Invert** or press CTRL/⌘-I.

Film Grain

100%

Grain 3

Highlight Area 0

Intensity 3

OK

Cancel

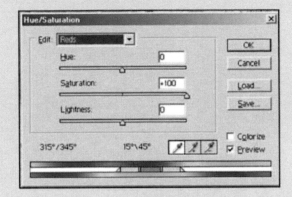

Here's what it should look like.

It's very light, but don't worry we'll take care of that.

10. Go to **Image > Adjustments > Hue/Saturation** or press Ctrl/⌘-U. Make sure Master is selected from the Edit drop-down menu (it is usually the default) and set the Hue to -180.

12. Invert the image again by choosing **Filter > Adjustments > Invert** or Ctrl/⌘-I. Take a look at the finished image – a great color infra-red effect.

11. Now select Red from the Edit drop-down menu. Set the Saturation to 100. Click OK.

9

Cross-processing effect

■
■
■

CMYK mode
Curves
Invert

Creating a cross-processed effect

Cross-processing is exactly what the word suggests. You take a roll of film, expose it and then process it in the "wrong" way, for example using transparency (positive) film to capture images, then having it developed into "regular" (C-41) print film, or using print film, then having it processed in E-6 (slide film chemicals). All of this creates color shifts and high contrast. Typically highlights become compressed in the yellow and magenta layers, so pure whites appear pinky-orange and shadow tones will contain a strong cyan/blue cast. Most of the mid to highlight details, like skin tones, get lost.

We are going to use the completed image from Chapter 7 and simulate the effects of cross-processing. This can be useful to give an image a ghostly or washed out feel.

1.   Open `model.tif`.

First we are going to convert the image to CMYK, as in this case we are assuming it is intended for print, and we need to play with the color channels. If you do this with your own images, you should ensure that they are fully color-corrected first.

2.   Go to **Image > Mode > CMYK Color**.

3.   Duplicate the 'background' layer and name it 'model'. Hide the 'background' layer.

4.   Select the Channels palette. We are going to adjust each color channel, which contains the images color information, rather than introducing new color information. This will make our final image look more authentic.

Activate the Yellow channel by highlighting it, and turn the eye icon for the CMYK channel on. (This enables you to see the color changes as they happen.)

9

215

5. With the Yellow channel selected, choose **Image >
    Apply Image**. Check the **Invert** box and set the
    blending mode to Hard Light at 45%.

The Apply Image facility allows you
to apply an image to itself using one
of the many blending modes provided in Photoshop 7. The non-destructive equivalent is to duplicate the
layer and apply the blending mode
and opacity adjustments in the
Layers palette.

The image should now look very yellow.

6. Repeat this on the Magenta channel, but take the
    opacity down to 37% and set the blending mode to
    Normal.

With the Magenta Channel modified your image will
look similar to this one.

7. Select the Cyan channel. Go to **Image > Apply
    Image** again, and this time don't check the Invert
    box, and set the blending mode to Multiply at
    100%.

The image should now begin looking cross-processed –
like the one below.

Next, we are going to use Curves to bring out the contrast of each channel, and to adjust the overall lighting of the image using the C, M, Y, and K channels.

8.   Let's start with the Cyan channel that we already have selected. Go to **Image > Adjust > Curves** or CTRL/⌘-M. First invert the brightness bar so the light end of the bar is on the right side by clicking on the arrows in the middle of it, as shown in the image below. It is important that your bar is set the same, so that you are putting the curves in the right direction to achieve the effect shown here. If you have the light end of the bar to the left, the curve would be reversed.

9.   Re-create the shape of the curve below. (Don't just enter the Input and Output values, as they are arbitrary values based on the shape of the Curve, and don't determine what the curve's shape will be.)

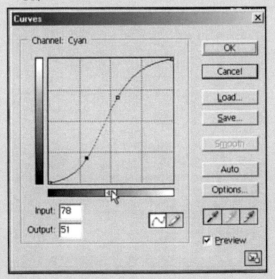

10.   Select the Magenta channel and go to **Image > Adjustments > Curves** or CTRL/⌘-M. As before, recreate the curve to match the one below. (The brightness bar should have stayed inverted – if not, invert it.)

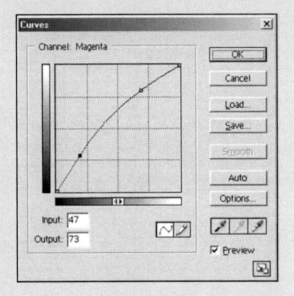

11.   Select the Yellow channel and again go to **Image > Adjust > Curves** and set your curve to match the one below. (The third point on the curve helps to control the curve of the line by serving as an anchor as one end affects the shape of the other.)

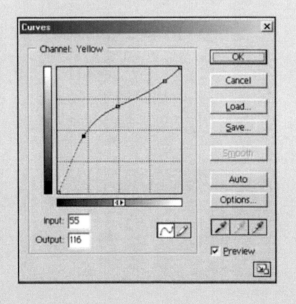

9

12. Select the Black channel. Once again open Curves and draw the curve shown below.

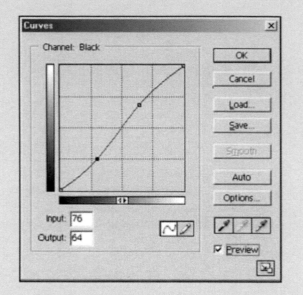

Here is the final image. Keep in mind that the above settings are only a guideline and may need to be adjusted according to individual images.

13. Finally, select the CMYK Channel. We are going to use Curves to adjust the contrast of the image. (If you prefer, you can use **Image > Adjust Brightness/Contrast**). Open up the Curves histogram and, one more time, mimic the curve pictured below.

9

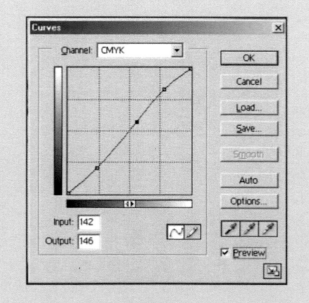

Chapter 10
Special Effects

Some great photographic techniques are produced using very time-consuming methods. Many of these effects are created by photographers making certain physical changes in the process of actually capturing the image they want. For example, painting with light requires a directional and continuous light source to be moved around the subject. Panning, on the other hand, is produced when the camera is moving at the same speed and in the same direction as the moving object being photographed.

As you can imagine, or may already know through experience, it is not always easy to come up with the desired results. Often it takes many attempts to get the picture right. But with the help of Photoshop, we can turn this workflow on its head, take our basic shot, and work with it to simulate these effects. This gives us far greater control over the final image, and of course the freedom to experiment and achieve what we want through that tried and tested method – trial and error. Never underestimate the freedom that CTRL/⌘-Z gives you.

In this chapter we are going to look at how to replicate some of these great photographic techniques using Photoshop. In particular we are going to paint with light, add a blur to a photo to simulate panning, imply forward motion using a motion blur, and produce a silhouette. In addition to this, we will take a look at how to attach text to your images that accentuates the message of the picture.

Painting with light

- Levels
- Brightness/Contrast
- Eraser tool
- Curves

Painting with light is a photographer's technique that employs a small, highly directional, continuous light source that is moved around a subject while your camera shutter is open. The result is a softly lit image with a dreamlike quality. This process takes time, as the light must be moved around in the right places while the rest of the shot is in total darkness. Exposure times are a guessing game at best. But thanks to Photoshop's layers and History palette, and its snapshot feature, we can re-create this technique with accuracy – and with the lights on!

1. Open up `tulip.tif`.

2. Duplicate the 'Background' layer and rename it 'Flowers'. Hide the visibility of the 'Background' layer.

The first thing we are going to do is adjust the Levels of the image to correct the density.

3. Go to **Image > Adjustments > Levels** or CTRL/⌘-L on the keyboard. Set the input shadow slider (located on the far left) to the first spike on the histogram to the left so that the corresponding Input Level display is at 36. This increases the shad-

ow tones in the image, thereby darkening the blacks.

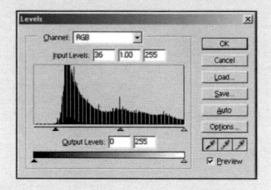

4. We are going to bump up the contrast of the 'Flowers' layer a bit to help intensify the colors, which will in turn add to the "wow" factor in the finished image. If your original image lacks contrast and punchy colors, or is "flat", the final effect will not be very striking. We really want the colors to jump out.

5. Choose **Image > Adjustments > Brightness/Contrast** Leave the Brightness and change the Contrast to 20.

10

6. Now duplicate the 'Flowers' layer and rename it 'Black'. We are going to darken this layer down to almost black to act as our darkened room, as we would have if we were real photographers painting with light.

7. Open up Levels again by choosing **Image > Adjustments > Levels** or CTRL/⌘-L on the keyboard.

   This time we are going to use the output sliders on the bottom of the box to darken the entire layer. By adjusting the output slider, we are changing the overall density of the image, in this case to almost completely black, and not the individual highlights, midtones, and shadows as we would using the Input Levels.

8. Move the highlight slider (the one on the right) over to the shadows end of the bar until the image is fairly dark – creating our darkened room. I have set the slider to 12 as shown below. You want to still be able to see the image so we know what we are working on, but dark enough to have some pure black areas.

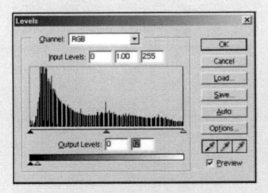

Your image should look very dark but with the silhouettes still visible.

9. To reveal the image beneath, select the Eraser tool and make sure your default brushes are loaded. Choose a Star brush set at around 130px. Turn the opacity down low to around 15%.

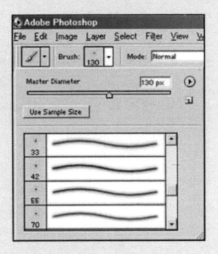

Now we are ready to begin the painting process.

10. Start to gradually erase the head of the main tulip in the middle of the image. Start at the bottom of the head sweeping upward with each stroke. By starting at the bottom of the flower head each time we are lightening it more than the rest of the flower. Brush around the tips of the flower to highlight them as well.

11. Take a snapshot of what you've done so far using the **Create new snapshot** icon at the bottom of the History palette. This way you can easily revert back to this point if you don't like what you've done to the next flower. Depending on how much you erased, your image should look similar to the one below.

10

12. Now start on the tulip on left side of this one that is located in the foreground. Use the upward sweeping motion to get the same effect as previously

13. Again, take a snapshot, in case you need to revert back.

14. Now select Dry brush 1 (one of the last brushes listed in the default set) and set the pixel size to 73. Keeping the Opacity set to around 15%, use this brush to lighten the rest of the flower heads in the image – going over each one a different number of times to give each a different lightness.

15. Switch back to the Star brush preset and this time choose a diameter of 100px. Brush over some of these flowers – some along the tips and some along the body, adjusting the opacity as you go to give more highlights, as shown in the image below.

16. Switch to a Soft Round brush with the diameter set to 27 and the opacity to around 20 we can start to bring out some of the stems. Begin with the main tulip. Do the same to the other main flowers adjusting the brush size as needed. Do as many passes as you'd like to bring them out.

Now we will lighten up the background a little to give it some texture and add some interest to it.

17. Choose **Image > Adjustments > Curves** or CTRL/⌘-M on the keyboard.

18. Set the highlights on the bar to the right side by clicking on the arrows in the middle of the bottom bar. Mimic the curve below to adjust the tones in the background so that some of the detail re-appears and it lightens slightly. Don't worry if it's not exact.

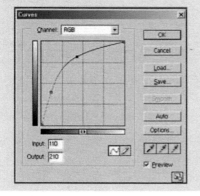

Remember that with Curves, you can't simply make two points on the line and enter in the Input and Output amounts that are shown above and expect to match the curve shown. The tones are determined by the shape of the curve and not visa versa.

Now take a look at the finished product. A soft image with a dream like quality.

Creative blur

- Magnetic
- Lasso
- Layers
- Blur filter

Panning is a great photographic technique. It's achieved by moving the camera in the same direction as a fast moving subject. The result is a somewhat sharp subject and a blurred background. The subject may not have been moving at a high speed when the picture was taken, but the final image makes it look like it was.

So what do you do if you have a frozen action shot, with a sharp background, and you want to give that suggestion of motion? With Photoshop, it's very easy. Let's jump right into to it and you'll see.

1. Open up `motorcycle.tif`. Not a bad image, but it could be much better without the distractingly sharp background. Plus motorcycles were meant to be photographed true to their nature – going fast!

2. As usual, start by duplicating the 'Background' layer. Rename it 'Bike' and turn off the visibility of the original 'Background' layer.

The first thing we need to do is to isolate the subject.

3. Select the Magnetic Lasso tool and set the Feather to 2px. Start selecting the bike and rider, switching to the Polygonal Lasso tool if you need to, to add

or subtract from the selection.

4. Once you have the bike and rider selected, choose **Select > Inverse**, or Ctrl/⌘-Shift-I on the keyboard, to make the background our selection.

10

5. Move the background to another layer by choosing **Layer > New > Layer Via Cut** or by pressing CTRL/⌘-SHIFT-J on the keyboard. Rename this new layer 'Blur', and then drag the 'Bike' layer above the 'Blur' layer.

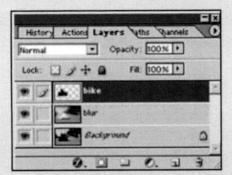

Now we are ready to begin creating that motion effect.

6. Select the 'Blur' layer. We are going to start creating motion here. To do this select **Filter > Blur > Motion Blur**. Set the Distance to 300px and the Angle to 4° to match the angle of the motorcycle.

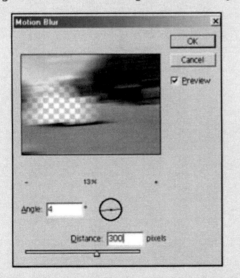

Wow! He's going fast now. Don't worry about the transparent pixels around the rider – we'll get to them right now.

7. Copy the background layer again and this time rename it 'Filler'. Your layer stacking order should look what is shown below.

We are going to blur the entire 'Filler' layer to fill in the open pixels.

8. Go to **Filter > Blur > Motion Blur** and make sure the settings are the same as we used earlier. (Distance 300px and Angle 4°.)

We need to eliminate the "cutout" effect that is happening.

9. Activate the 'Bike' layer. Select the Blur tool and choose a soft edge brush with a diameter of 17px. With the Strength set to 100%, gently drag the brush along all the cutout edges of the bike and rider to soften them. Make sure to blur the background that shows through the tire rims too.

10

He's coming right for us

- Lasso
- Gaussian Blur
- Radial Blur
- History palette

Now let's try another blurring technique. Our goal this time is to blur out the background of the image to make the bike and rider really come off the screen. We want to imply some motion here so that the image doesn't look like it's been completely frozen. Using traditional photographic techniques, to capture motion in the image we would have to either use a slow shutter speed resulting in the rider being blurred and the background staying sharp; or use a zoom lens and zoom-in on the rider as the shutter is open. If you have ever tried this, you'll soon see that both traditional techniques don't really compare to what we can create with Photoshop.

1.   Open Rider.tif.

2.   As usual, duplicate the 'Background' layer. Rename it 'Bike'. Turn off the visibility of the 'Background' layer.

3.   Select the bike and rider as we did in the above example using the Lasso tools to get your selection.

4.   Go to **Select > Inverse** or press CTRL/⌘-SHIFT-I on the keyboard.

10

229

5. Select **Layer > New > Layer Via Cut**, or CTRL/⌘-SHIFT-J on the keyboard, to move the background onto a new layer. Name it 'Blur.'

6. Drag the 'Bike' layer above the 'Blur' layer.

7. Activate the 'Blur' Layer. Go to **Filter > Blur > Gaussian Blur**. Zoom out with the minus symbol on the left of the preview image to view where the effect will be applied. Set the Radius to 23.2. Again, don't worry about the empty pixels surrounding the subject, we'll fix that.

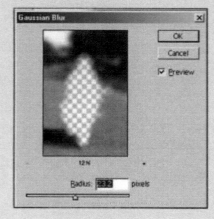

8. Still on the 'Blur' layer, we are now going to create the illusion of motion. Choose **Filter > Blur > Radial Blur**. Set the Amount to 100, the Blur Method to Zoom, and the Quality at either Good or Best. Best will take longer for the filter to apply.

> We applied the Gaussian Blur first to soften the effect of the Radial Blur, which produces very sharp straight unrealistic lines. The aim, as always, is to make the image look as real as possible.

9. Now choose the History Brush tool and select a soft edge brush set at around 40px. Set the opacity to 100% and turn on the Airbrush option, which is located on the History Brush's Options bar.

    We now need to choose our source for the brush. To do this, open the History palette. Make sure that the History Brush icon is turned on beside the Bike.tif image at the top of the palette. Be careful not to click on the actual image as this will cause you to revert back.

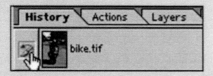

10. Here our goal is to make part of the foreground sharper so the front tyre doesn't look like it's floating. Besides the rider is moving towards us, he's already zoomed past the background at incredible speed, he hasn't reached the foreground yet!

    To accomplish this, begin brushing the road in the foreground, restoring the sharpness. As you reach the front of the tire, turn the opacity down to around 30%. Taking advantage of the Airbrush option, begin sweeping the brush over the road up to the light, gradually leaving more blur as you go. You want any sharpness to end around the middle of the bike's position on the road.

11. Next, copy the 'Background' layer again and rename it 'Fill'. We are going to blur the entire layer to fill in the transparent pixels around the bike. Choose to **Filter > Blur > Gaussian Blur** and set it to 23.2 pixels as you did above.

12. Apply the Radial Blur to this layer as well to ensure the pixels match up seamlessly. **Filter > Blur > Radial Blur**. Amount: 100, Blur Method: Zoom, Quality: Good.

    The empty pixels are now filled with a blur to match the background. All that is left to do is subtly blur the edges of the bike and rider, to help them blend better with the background and avoid a cutout effect.

13. Choose the Blur tool and select a soft edge brush with a diameter of 35px, with the opacity set to 100%. Move the brush gently over the outside edges of the bike and rider until you are satisfied with the result.

10

Take a look at the final image. The rider and bike are no longer lost in the background. Now they jump off the screen. By using the Radial Blur in combination with the Gaussian Blur we have implied a bit of motion that we would not have been able to capture on film using traditional techniques.

10

Type effects

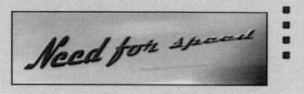

- Text tool
- Layer Styles
- Rotate
- Skew

Okay, so far we've spent the entire book using Photoshop to do some pretty cool things to images, but have you thought about using similar techniques to produce text effects? These effects are great for creating professional products and promotional pieces. Think of different magazine covers that you like – the text still jumps off the page at the reader regardless of the image. Let's have a look at some type effects that we can create easily that look like they'd take hours to create. (At one point I'm sure they did!)

1. Open your final panned/blurred image from the first motorcycle blur effect or fast_rider.tif. We are going to add some text to the image. Imagine that we are creating a poster and we need a little bit of text to advertise our product, in this case the bike and/or lifestyle of a typical rider.

2. Select the Text tool and choose a font that you like. I've chosen Magneto bold set at 24pt as I find this font fits well with the movement of the image. I have also chosen a red for the color to help make it stand out against the background. (Click on the color box in the Type tool's Options bar and choose a red you like or enter in color #F70505 (R: 247, G: 5, B: 5).

3. Now click the on the upper left corner of the image and take note of how Photoshop automatically creates a new layer for the type. Type in *Need for Speed*. As you type, Photoshop automatically

names the layer accordingly. This layer is now called 'Need for speed'.

4. The first thing that we are going to do to the text is warp it in such a way as to imply motion in it while still matching the image's background movement. Choose the Warp Text icon from the Type tool Options bar and take a moment to play with the different effects.

5. I ended up choosing the Fish effect as it let me change the shape of the text to make it look like it is trailing off and still give a little extra shape over the other options. I set the Bend to +19%, the Horizontal Distortion to –46%, and the Vertical Distortion to +2%.

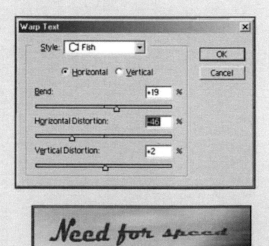

Now we are going to apply some styles to our text to give it some depth using Layer Effects.

Layer Effects are *live effects*, which means that they are applied to the layer but can be modified or removed at any time, unless you flatten the image. (They work like adjustment layers.)

10

6. Select Layer Styles by either clicking on the *f* icon located at the bottom of the Layers palette and choosing Blending Options, or by right-clicking on the text layer and choosing Blending Options.

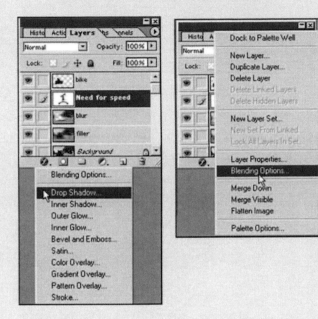

It may take a few seconds for the window to open.

> A quick note about using Layer Styles before we go any further. When selecting a style, click on the word, not the check box. This displays the settings for that style, which you can edit. If you only check the box next to the style, the style is selected, but at the default settings.

7. Choose the Drop Shadow. Move the Layer Styles box on your screen so you can see the text we are modifying and make sure the Preview option is turned on.

Feel free to take a moment here to play with the different options to see how they affect your text – it can all be easily undone. Change the angle of the shadow, the Distance and Spread etc. Click on the drop-down options in Contours and see how each one changes the drop shadow.

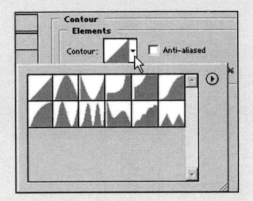

8. Now hold down the ALT/OPT key to change the Cancel button into a Reset button and reset the window to the default settings. Select the Drop Shadow again. For this example, I'm leaving it at the default settings, but feel free to set them to however you like.

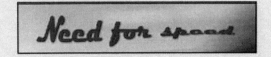

The Drop Shadow has given the text some depth.

9. Now choose Bevel and Emboss. (Remember to select the text, not the check box so we can adjust the settings.) This option gives the text itself a 3-D look.

10

10. Select Inner Bevel and set the Shadow Opacity to 100%. I have set my Altitude to 6° and have also changed the color of my shadow to a darker red by clicking on the color box. To match the shade that I am using enter in color # 870303 or R: 135, G: 3, B: 3.

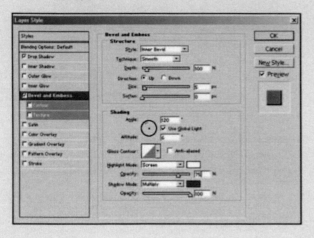

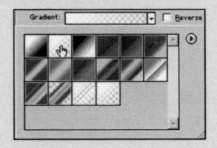

12. The Angle is set to 180° so that the gradient will be applied evenly across the text. Set the Scale to 117%. (The Scale adjusts where the gradient blends in the object.)

Here is a good time to mention that if you are not happy with your settings, such as the Bevel and Emboss, and want to return to the defaults, don't use the Reset option. If you choose Reset, you will be resetting everything, including the Drop Shadow. If you need to, the easiest way would be to turn off Bevel and Emboss style and click OK to accept the ones you like the settings for, such as Drop Shadow and Outer Glow. Then reopen the Layer Styles dialog – those you left unselected will revert to their defaults.

13. Click OK to accept the settings and take a look at the Layers palette. We've done quite a bit to our text, very easily.

Note that each of the styles we applied is listed within the layer. To edit these at any time, simply double-click on the specific effect. You can also turn the visibility of these effects on and off. (If the visibility is turned off on an effect when the image is flattened, it will be not be applied. The same is true for layers, by the way.)

11. The last thing we are going to do in this palette is apply a Gradient Overlay. Click on the word Gradient Overlay to bring up the settings. What we are doing here is applying a gradient to our text layer so that the end of it starts to fade slightly.

I've left the Blending Mode at Normal, but changed the Opacity to 81%. I selected the *Foreground to Transparent* gradient by clicking on the drop-down arrow.

10

Take a look at the text now – it no longer looks one-dimensional.

We are almost finished. We are going to finish up this effect by slightly skewing and rotating the text using the Transform options.

14. Choose **Edit > Transform > Skew**. Drag the top line of the bounding box that has appeared to the right, skewing the text the direction of the images background motion.

Drag it to the right as much as you'd like or enter in the settings below to match the example.

X: 523.1 Y: 102.4 W: 100.0 H: 100.0 0.0 H: -29.8 V: 0.0

15. Finally choose **Edit > Transform > Rotate** and grab an edge on the bounding box to rotate the text to match the angle of where the sky meets the ground or type –2.3 for the Angle.

X: 523.1 Y: 102.4 W: 100.0 H: 100.0 -2.3 H: 0.0 V: 0.0

The text looks much more at home than a simple caption would have.

10

Type masking

- Fill
- Layers
- Masks

1. Open your source image – I'm going to use the painted tulips from earlier in this chapter (light-en.tif).

2. Duplicate the 'Background' layer and rename the new layer 'Tulips'. Turn the visibility of the 'Background' layer off.

3. Create a new layer using the Create a new layer icon at the bottom of the Layers palette and name it 'White'. Choose **Edit > Fill** and fill it with white.

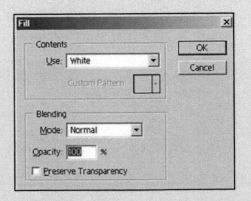

4. Drag the 'White' layer below the 'Tulips' layer.

5. Activate the 'Tulips' layer. Select the Type tool and Right/CTRL-click on the tool to show the other tool options. Choose the Horizontal Type Mask tool.

T Horizontal Type Tool	T
IT Vertical Type Tool	T
Horizontal Type Mask Tool	T
Vertical Type Mask Tool	T

6. Type the word Tulips. Notice the mask that appears.

7. Change the font to whatever you like and make it large enough to almost cover from side to side. I've chosen Showcard Gothic, a fun bulky font, set at 80 pt. This will allow for a lot of the image to come through.

10

| T | T | Showcard Gothic | Regular | T | 80 pt | aa | Sharp | |

8. Choose the Warp Text option box, located on the Type tool Options bar, and chose an effect you like. I chose Bulge, set to 80% in order to really maximize the size of the font so a lot of the image will show through.

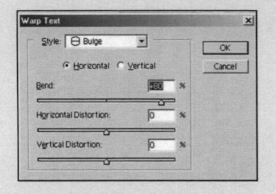

9. Now slowly move the mouse away from the text until the mouse turns into the Move icon. Re-position the text so that it's in the middle of the image. Click on the Checkmark icon on the Type tool Options bar or click anywhere on the image to "commit any current edits."

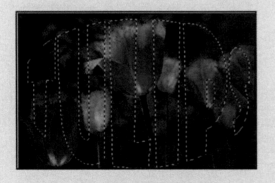

10. Select **Layer > Add Layer Mask > Reveal Selection**. It's just that easy!! Try doing this with a portrait and use the subject's name to create the mask.

Silhouettes

- Extract
- Levels
- Layers
- Free Transform tool

Okay so far we've learned some pretty cool things using Photoshop. So I say how about something a little more old fashioned? Silhouettes date from a time before cameras, when skilled craftspeople would cut the shape of someone's profile onto card, or trace a shadow.

Clearly a silhouette requires a degree of shape in the original image, hence the traditional use of the profile. We can, of course, choose any shape that would make sense – a couple hand in hand at distance would be just as clichéd, for example.

1. Open your choice of source image and save it under a different name. It will help to have a contrasting color in the background.

2. Open the Extract tool using **Filter > Extract**.

3. Zoom in on your subject and select the brush. Make it as small as you think you can get away with (using the Tool options panel on the right) then drag it around the edges of your subject. When you come to hair, ensure that you paint over all the areas in which there are individual strands of hair.

You can zoom out (and get the opposite of all the tools on the left of the Extract window) by clicking and holding the ALT/OPT key as you click.

4. When you're finished switch to the Fill tool to fill all the areas of your subject you wish to keep.

10

5. Use the Edge Touchup tool and Cleanup tool to go around problem areas of your image. ALT/OPT-clicking with the Edge Touchup tool fills the original back, just clicking removes areas. Remember you can change the brush size whenever it suits, and zoom in and out.

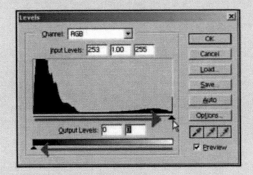

6. Once you're happy click OK and Photoshop will extract your subject onto a transparent background.

7. Now might be a good moment to save your image, which can easily be placed on another background. Here, however, we'll press on...

8. Open the Levels tool by clicking **Image > Adjustments > Levels...** or CTRL/⌘-L.

9. Drag the shadows slider all the way from right to left, which should place the whole image into shadow.

10. Just to be sure, drag the lower right slider all the way to ensure an image based entirely on black. Click OK.

The advantage of this method is that we now have our silhouette with alpha-channel edges that are more believable than the alternative method – to select our subject and fill her with black. This would lose important details like hair, and create a sharper edge.

11. All that remains is to open a background image, click once again on our silhouette to make her the active layer then drag her from the Layers palette onto the final background.

12. You can drag your new layer over your background to find a suitable spot. You may also find that you need the Free Transform tool (CTRL/⌘-T) to scale your subject to fit the background image.

 You can flip your silhouette along the horizontal without affecting the apparent reality, as there is no detail inside it.

10

10

10

Chapter 11
Preparing Images for Print and Optimizing for the Web

Finally, after all our toil, we want to show off our new creations. Of course, you can get your friends to come and look at them on your screen and marvel, but most of the time we need to distribute our image in some way, and this usually comes down to the web, or print.

Each destination has its own set of drawbacks and difficulties. Like every other stage of your image process, what we would like to do is to homogenize, as far as possible, our intentions for our image, the resultant piece of work, and how it is perceived by our audience.

We'll look at color management and how it can help and hinder our attempts at perfection – in fact here is where all that theory in Chapter 1 will really pay off.

We'll also have a look at a couple of web projects. Sadly there is no room for an in depth discussion of building a web site with Photoshop – that's probably a book in itself – what we will see in this chapter is no see how to slice complex images for optimum download, or get Photoshop to produce a web gallery for you.

No discussion of these methods would be complete without an in depth look at the file format, which we've attempted to make as succinct as possible using easy to read tables. In other words, by absorbing the information in this chapter, you should have enough of a grounding in the assorted output methods o publish your work. That said, always remember to ask your clients, or your printing house, for any special requirements.

From light to dark

Traditionally, we'd want to print out our images, so let's start there, preparing our images for print.In the first chapter we discussed the evolutionary process of your photography. Let's recap quickly. When we take our images, using our traditional camera, the film in our camera captures the light using light sensitive chemicals on the film.

This is an interpretation of the scene, not the actual scene itself. So for instance if we take the picture really quickly or jerkily, we will get an image that is not a true representation of the scene. Capturing the scene exactly as it really is can obviously be really difficult, and a lot of skill goes into this part of the process. Skill often equates to trial and error, with a heavy emphasis on the error part. For this reason a lot of people are switching to digital cameras, as your errors are a lot cheaper.

The basic point to observe here is that even if you're a really talented photographer, it's quite plausible that the photograph you take will not exactly resemble the scene in front of you. So already at this point the original has been altered.

Also, you get good film and bad film. Sometimes the different chemicals on different films can be superior or inferior in quality.

So the film itself may not be perfectly accurate at capturing the scene. On a digital camera, the "film" (plate) that is used cannot be replaced. You can't just run out and buy a better film – you're stuck with the one that comes with the camera – a point worth noting when you decide to buy one. Back with traditional film, there is also the development stage. That is a chemical process, which can obviously also vary in quality, so once again the interpretation of the scene can get further from the original.

More importantly, at the point of development and printing, light is converted to ink. In Chapter 1 we discussed the different color models, specifically **additive** and **subtractive**. Remember, we said that **additive** color was created when you shone two or more beams of light together. So if you shine red and green lights together, your resultant is a yellow light. This resultant light is lighter and brighter than the lights you started with. The more light we add, the brighter the resultant light.

The opposite is true for **subtractive** color, the process used when you mix paint or ink together (for instance). The more you mix, the darker your result (assuming you're not using white paint that is). Basically, the more color you take away, the lighter the result would be.

At this stage, after much possible color interpretation/change we have our initial print. But we haven't even started working on it yet!

Today's development/processing places are often sophisticated enough to be able to subtly adjust the balance of chemicals used when developing your photograph, which means you can reprint your images if you're not happy with the way the color or intensity looks. So using your own judgment will often help fix any color inaccuracies that have crept in.

After all that, only now is it time to scan the photograph in, which is a further interpretation of the colors. A scanner works in much the same way as a digital camera, capturing light, which is reflected off the image, and storing it digitally. Because your photograph doesn't actually glow, the scanner produces its own light – as a photocopier does.

Once again, an interpretation of the color has to be made, and it is very common for errors in the color and light intensity to appear at this stage. Obviously a digital camera would have cut out many of these potentially hazardous steps, but not to worry; digital cameras have their own problems in interpreting the original light source, so we're all pretty much in the same boat.

Basically what this boils down to is the image we have just obtained – whether by digital or analog means – in all likelihood differs quite substantially from the original scene. That's ok, we're expecting it.

11

In Chapter 2 we saw how these initial problems could be cleared up fairly easily. As we discussed then, we are altering the image on a perceptual level. The scanned in or digitally dumped photograph represents the image in its purest state. Whatever we do to it from there on will degrade the quality – in other words information will be lost from the image. Yes, the color or contrast of the image might not resemble our original scene, but this is a judgment on our part.

For instance, the image might not have enough contrast, so we slap in a brightness/contrast adjustment and that's that. But some of the fine gradations of color/light will in all likelihood have been lost and replaced with a uniformly darker tone. From a perceptual point of view this wouldn't bother us – the image in all likelihood now bears a closer resemblance to the original scene. But the more times we alter the image, to get it closer to the way we perceive the original to have been, the more information we can destroy along the way.

My point? If you want a high quality result, try and keep your modifications to a minimum. For instance, don't add a hue/saturation adjustment layer, then a brightness/contrast one and then, if you're still not happy with the result, another hue/saturation. Instead, go back to your original hue/saturation adjustment layer and see if you can alter it to suit your now changed needs brought about by the brightness/contrast changes.

Changing the brightness and contrast of the image is going to unavoidably change the color, and visa versa. You can quite easily get into a vicious loop this way, adding more and more adjustment layers. This might suit your purposes, but just remember that in all likelihood the quality of the print will suffer.

In a similar vein to the differences in cameras and film repro, computer monitors and display cards also display color differently.

As mentioned in Chapter 1, using color management systems can largely overcome this problem. Let's have a closer look at them.

Color management systems

Before we go any further, it's worth noting that it's a good idea to keep the colors we use as consistent as possible. After our previous discussion, this seems a bit like a futile exercise. Why keep the colors consistent when there are so many parts of the process that we cannot control?

Although many color changes have in all likelihood taken place up until now, at least if we manage to get the color right between the monitor and the page, we should be okay. A color management system ensures just this. Although all printers print differently, even ones of the same make and model, using an ICC (International Color Consortium) color profile means that the printer is sent specific instructions on how to reproduce the color. Let's take a closer look at the process of setting this up:

Using **Edit > Color Settings** gives us the following dialog box:

11

The dialog box is broken down into four different areas – let's take a look at each.

Working Spaces

We have previously discussed the RGB and CMYK color modes, which represent two main categories of color spaces. The main problem creeps in when we try to switch from the one to the other. This is mainly because the range (gamut) of colors (or *color space*) differs from the one to the other. This means that there are some colors that you can get on your monitor that just can't be printed.

Throughout our process of capturing a scene and displaying/printing it, we are dealing with different ranges of colors – all of them subsets of the range available in nature, which is both superior and much larger.

The gamuts of the RGB and CMYK color spaces are different enough to cause us a bit of a headache. Although the RGB gamut has a larger range than CMYK, it cannot display all of the CMYK colors, so it works both ways.

Now as we know, different pieces of hardware have varying gamuts. Two identical monitors may produce quite a different range of RGB colors.

When we create and use a working space profile we are establishing a color space that will be consistent independent of the device we use. The image will look the same regardless of what computer we look at it on, or what printer we use to print it out – assuming that they are using the same working space profile.

There are a number of flavors to choose from, so let's look at a few of the RGB ones:

Type	Description	Recommendation
Monitor RGB	This sets the RGB working space to your current monitor's working space. This means that everything will appear as it normally does on your monitor.	Use this setting when other devices in your production line won't have color management
sRGB IEC61966-2.1	Bit of a mouthful! This profile reflects the average monitor and is often the default for many home and small office scanners and ink jet printers	Perfect for publishing to the web. Not so great for printing as it has a fairly limited gamut
ProPhoto RGB	Uses a very large range of RGB colors taking into account the entire range of photographic materials	Great for inkjet photo printers and digital dye subs. This working space should accurately display pretty much any image from a digital camera. Not so great for traditional printing, as the discrepancy between it and most CMYK working spaces is large
Adobe RGB	Uses a more limited, but still fairly large range of RGB	Use this working space when you are going to be converting to CMYK. Great if you're going to be printing with a lot of color

Similarly, you can decide on a CMYK color space to use, and often you will want to load one for your specific printer, so that whatever you see on the screen will pretty much come out of the printer looking the same. So depending on what you want to accomplish you will use a different working space.

Color Management Policies

If you are planning to use color management, there are a few scenarios that you might like to consider:

Scenario	Recommendation
If your workflow consists of different devices such as cameras, computers and printers.	Use color management if the devices support it. It's pointless to set up and convert things to a specific workspace only to pass the project on to the printers who phone you back and say "Uh we got your email about the color space. How much space do you want in the color? We thought you wanted all the dots printed closely together…"
If your primary task is to print something.	Try your best to use a color management system, especially if it's important to you to accurately represent the colors.
If you're publishing to the web.	Your best bet is using a conservative color management policy such as sRGB or none at all. With the wide variety of computers out there, many of which won't be using color management, you're pretty much holding a candle to the wind.

You have two options when opening a file with color management turned on:

11

Preserve embedded profiles

When opening a file that does not match your current color working space, Photoshop will match the colors of an RGB file to ones from your working space, at the expense of the numerical values.

So let's say we're opening up an image that is just red, of RGB 182,15,15, and we have a fairly light monitor. Without color management, the color will appear much brighter than it should. The color management system will therefore attempt to display this color correctly and drop the RGB values to something like RGB 172,15,15 to compensate for this. This means that on our bright monitor the color will have different numerical values, but will look the same.

With a CMYK file, Photoshop will preserve the numerical values at the expense of the way the colors look. Because we are in all likelihood wanting to print a CMYK file, the numerical values are more important than the way the image looks on the screen. So that same red in CMYK, which is 20,100,100,12 will end up looking brighter on our monitor, but will print out the same as intended by the person that sent us the file.

Convert to Working RGB

This does exactly the opposite of the above. Instead of preserving the way the image looks, it is converted to the current color space being used.

Conversion options

So how does Photoshop go about converting from one working space to another? Using the Adobe Engine (recommended), we have four options:

Type	Recommendation
Perceptual	This conversion method will preserve the relationship between source colors. Use when you have a large gamut of source colors which you'd like to keep. So the colors might not exactly match up, but you'll get the most realistic looking image.
Saturation	This conversion method will disregard matching up colors in favor of producing a saturated result – useful when you're doing presentations and you want a nice rich look and feel.
Relative	Using the LAB color model to convert colors, this system tries to match up media specific colors and at the same time preserve the white point. : the This means that the image will look pretty much the same and have the same luminosity, especially when you know that most of the colors have the same gamut from source to destination.
Absolute	Similar to relative, but this system takes the LAB values of each independent of the media they come from and irrespective of the white points of each. This would be used where you're trying to produce very accurate color results – such as for company logos.

Advanced controls

Caution: do not try using these settings without a safety net and the presence of a qualified paramedic! These settings can be useful if you'd like to display a range of colors larger than is possible for your monitor. By desaturating the entire gamut, this can be made possible, but what you will now be viewing will no longer match what spews out of your printer.

11

You can also take specific gammas into account when blending RGB colors which means a more accurate use of half tones at the edge of color areas, but few other applications are able to replicate this.

Making your images ready to print – color separations and resolutions

Now that you have all your color management issues firmly under control it's time to get your image ready to print.

So we've taken a photograph, made adjustments to it and attached a color profile to allow for accurate printing. Usually, we have converted to CMYK mode to see how the image is going to look. Remember that it's useful to have an ICC profile loaded for the printer that you're going to be using so that you can accurately assess the color that is going to be printed. When you're printing something, CMYK color management can help quite a bit. Or, if you prefer, and can afford the time and ink, there's always the tried and trusted method of printing the same image 43 times, making minor changes each time until you're happy with the result.

Most printers will want the proofs in 300 dpi (dots per inch) or higher.

The more dots (in a square inch), the better your picture will print (the higher the resolution).

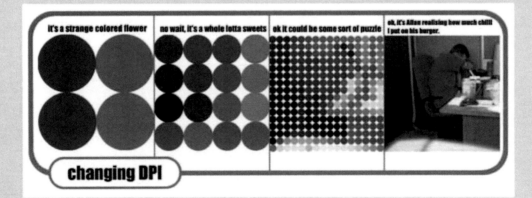

Publishing to the web

There is far less of a headache when publishing to the web. But while color management is less of an issue, file size and type suddenly becomes really important.

It's great to display a fantastic quality image on the web, but if it takes 3 hours to download, not many people are going to see your masterpiece. Instead you have to select the most appropriate file format from the web favorites.

File Type	Description	When To Use	Drawbacks
JPG	This file type uses a good compression algorithm to save the file. This does mean that image quality is sacrificed in favor of file size, but often a pleasing middle ground can be found.	When you've got lots of colors in your image this is a good format to use.	Some of the image information/quality will be lost. This file type cannot save or display transparency.
GIF	Instead of using a compression algorithm to reduce file size, this file format reduces the number of colors available in the gamut to 256. It dithers (uses a checkered pattern of two or more colors) to display colors that have been removed from the gamut. It doesn't always do this very well however, especially when trying to reproduce fine gradients – which end up as bands of changing color.	When you've got a fairly small range of colors in your image this is a good bet. Because you can cut out the colors that you don't need, you can greatly reduce the file size. Also, this format can display transparency – but in a rather primitive way; something is either rendered as transparent or not, there's no semi-transparency.	Not good on images where there are lots of colors.
BMP	This is the standard image format for Windows and DOS, and can save a wide gamut of colors.	If you either want a high quality result and aren't too concerned about file size, or want to ensure that the person can view the image on a PC, this is the way to go. Handy as a desktop backdrop for PCs.	Produces a fairly large file size when saved in normal mode and doesn't have the best compression algorithm when you try making it smaller.
PNG	This is a new image format and attempts to overcome the limitations of the other file types. PNG images can handle complex transparency and can be saved with or without image degradation.	Great if you need variable transparency and don't want to lose image quality.	Not so great if you want a small file size. Complex transparency and high image quality comes at a rather dear price in this case. Also, some older web browsers don't support this file type

Photoshop 7.0 comes bundled with ImageReady – the perfect tool to create web images. This software allows you to view both the original and proposed optimized image at the same time, which gives you the power to decide how much image degradation is acceptable. For example, have a look at the possibilities of saving the following image, which I took in the Kruger National Park:

11

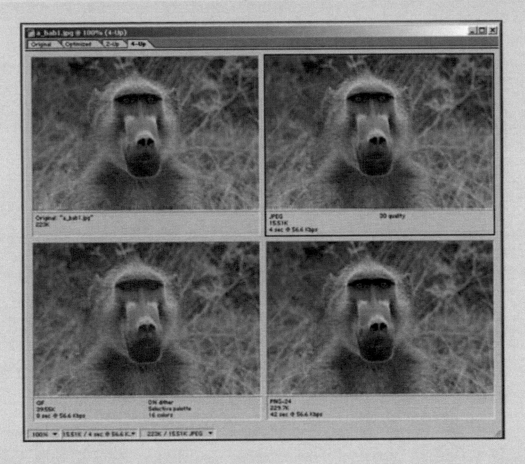

I've chosen the four-up option from the tabs at the top, which as you can see splits the display into 4. You can click on any one of these 4 to select it, and then change the settings. When you do this, you can make a comparison between different settings in terms of quality and file size. Here I have got 1 original (top left) and the rest are possible optimizations (JPG, GIF and PNG). Underneath each image is the type of file extension, the file size (the jpg won here with a file size of 15.51K) and roughly how long it will take to download this image on a web page using a standard 56.6 Kbps modem.

It's hardly even possible to discern the image loss between the JPG and the original. As you can see, even though we are only using 16 colors to create a GIF, it is still a 40K image, and the loss of image quality and patterning as a result of the compensating dither means that it is clearly not the right file format to use for such a color intensive image.

Strangely enough, the PNG is actually bigger than the original – it uses a lossless format to save the file – which is less efficient than the original JPG file.

11

Web gallery

A nice and convenient way of quickly publishing your images to the web, is to use the built in Web Photo Gallery option. It's really easy to use – pick from a variety of styles and browse for a directory on your computer where you saved all the images you want to include in the gallery:

1. Place all the images that you wish to publish in a folder somewhere on your hard drive.

2. Create a destination folder, where you want your gallery to end up.

3. Click **File > Automate > Web Photo Gallery...**

4. Select the folder in which you saved your images by clicking the 'Browse' button.

5. Select your destination folder using the button below.

6. The options allow you to automatically resize the images in your specified folder and even change their size to constrain them to certain proportions. You can currently see the settings for the banner, which will be displayed at the top of the page. Cycle through all the options and fill in the details as you see fit (the preview on the right will give you a rough idea of the page format, but doesn't use your pictures).

7. Once you've clicked on OK, Photoshop will create all the HTML and layouts necessary to create a fully functional web gallery, complete with thumbnails of each image, which you can click on. Here's what the end result looks like:

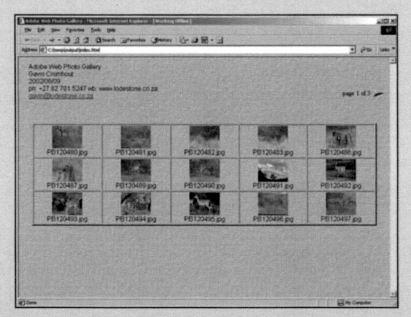

8. All that remains for you to do is upload the destination directory where Photoshop saved all the files, and try and explain why you took so many pictures of a stupid antelope when there were far more interesting things like lions roaming about. I'd give you the answer too (complete with story about baboon riding around on the roof of the car), but you probably wouldn't believe me.

11

Advanced optimization

- ImageReady
- Slice tool
- Slice palette
- Save Optimized

Sometimes you'll want to do more than just upload your images, you might want them to be part of a website design. Although we've looked at which file formats to use, sometimes it isn't so simple. What about an image that has a whole lot of flat color space with some complex color areas – like a person leaning against a wall?

We know that GIFs work best with flat color, which is perfect for the wall – but a GIF won't work at all well for the person. Conversely, it seems an awful waste to make the entire image a JPG. Enter the hybrid image. Have a look at the image below:

The image contains both large areas of flat and gradient color. Saving this entire image just as a JPG or a GIF wouldn't be a good idea. If we chose GIF, we'd either end up with a huge file size or have to sacrifice a lot of the color. If we chose JPG, we'd also have a problem with file size, or we'd really have to sacrifice image quality.

What we can do for the web, is break the image up into smaller parts and save them as different file types, thus gaining the best of both worlds – GIF **and** JPG.

1. Export the file to ImageReady, Photoshop's sister application. You can do this by clicking on the button at the bottom of the Toolbar, or by pressing CTRL/⌘-SHIFT-M.

2. The first thing we need to do is create slices. We need to delineate areas that will be saved as the different file types, and optimized separately.

To achieve this we use the **Slice** tool.

3. This tool works a lot like the Rectangular Marquee tool. It shares its docking space with the Slice Select tool, so using the left mouse button, hold down the icon until you get a fly out box and select the Slice tool if the Select tool is currently showing.

4. Drag a marquee over the area you want to slice up and release. Let's start by slicing the image into two – using the dotted line down the middle of the image as the boundary:

11

255

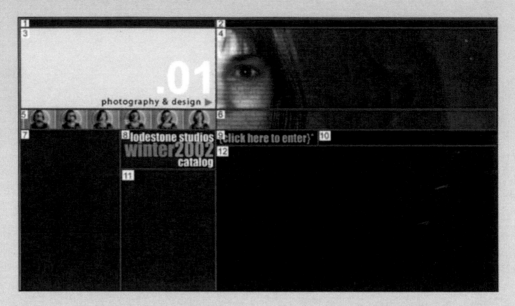

Notice the yellow border with tiny toggles along each line. If necessary, we can change the shape of the slice at a later date by dragging these toggles. Also notice that everything except the selected slice is grayed out.

In the top left hand corner of the slice is a tiny 01, telling us that this is slice number 1. We can see an 02 at the top of the right hand slice. So we have effectively cut the image into two pieces. Let's slow down a little bit and plan how we are going to optimize this image.

This plan is based on our appraisal of the different elements of the image. What we're trying to do here is separate the flat color areas from the gradient areas. So areas 1,2,3,7,8,9,10,11 and 12 have only flat color, while areas 4,5 and 6 are composed of gradient color.

The drawback with slicing thing up is that for each slice we add about 1k to the final result. That's just the way it is - so try keep the number of slices to a minimum. With this in mind, could we improve our slices?

Well slices 1 and 2 are the same, so we can join them together to make one slice. Have a look at slices 7,8 and 11. The reason they're not just one slice is that slice 8 has many more colors than the other two. So we can optimize slices 7 and 11 each as a 2-color GIF and slice 8 as a 6-color GIF. Why can't we create a 1-color GIF? If we're using a color that isn't available in the limited 256-color GIF palette, we need to emulate the color using a checkered pattern of two different colors.

Are the combined sizes of the three slices (7, 11 and 8) smaller than if we had just optimized them all as one 6-color gif? This is another thing to check, but for the sake of this example, we're going to assume that this IS the case here.

The same argument goes for slices 9,10 and 12, although in this case we specifically want to delineate slice 9, as we want to make this slice into a button later on.

And what about slice 3? Shouldn't we slice this area up into a few slices for the same reason as slices 7,8 and 11? In this case the area is a lot smaller, so there's a pretty good chance that we will actually be increasing the collective file size if we add slices than just going for the whole area as a 6-color gif. So we have:

11

Have another look at the image where we made our first slice. Notice that the slice on the right is gray. At this point we'd only made one slice. The slice on the right (slice 02) is the remainder. This is therefore an automatic slice – the size of which is dependent on slice 1 – so if we resize slice 1, slice 2 will automatically resize with it.

If you want to make this area into a real slice that can be resized independently of slice 1, simply use the slice tool over this area. Luckily the slice tool snaps to existing slices!

When I created slices 6, 7 and 11 all that was required was for me to create slice 7 – Photoshop automatically created slices 6 and 11. Because of the limitations of the web and the way images and files are displayed, we have to stick to a grid format. This means that we can cut any of our rectangles into smaller rectangles – but we cannot create any other shapes:

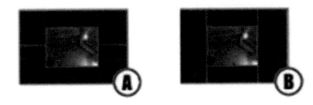

We can't slice up the image using method A, as it creates non-rectangular shapes. Method B, on the other hand, doesn't.

Photoshop will automatically create your slices according to method B, when it has to automatically fill in the remainder slices.

Optimizing your slices

1. Let's switch over to the optimized tab at the top of our project document.

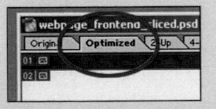

This will allow us to see each slice according to how we optimize it. Just to the right of it is a 2-Up tab – useful when you want to compare the sliced version to the original face to face.

2. Now, using the Slice Select tool (with the mouse, hold down the Slice tool icon to get access to the Slice Select tool or press the K key), we are going to select the slice with the face on it (slice 3).

Have a look at your Optimize palette:

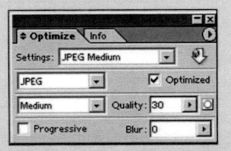

3. This palette allows you to set how you want to optimize each slice. The settings drop down box gives you a choice of a number of useful 'most used' settings. In this case, the JPEG Medium is a pretty good start, so select that. Notice that at the bottom of the image we can see how big (file size wise) this slice will be.

11

So the size of the entire image (all the slices added together) is roughly 22K and this particular slice is just over 7K. It's a good idea to constantly keep an eye on these figures. 22K is pretty good for the entire image, so we might be able to be a bit more lenient on our current slice to increase the quality – seeing as how it's the most graphic area.

Next we're going to tackle the slice immediately to the left, the one that says photography and design. For this slice we decided on using the GIF file type. You have quite a bit more control over modifying a GIF, not just the quality slider that you have on a JPG.

4. Select the 'GIF 32 No Dither' to start with. We clearly have less than 32 colors in our slice, so we can be assured that we haven't lost any information by trimming the palette down.

5. Choose the Selective palette, which means that the 256 colors available to a GIF are made up out of colors that the human eye can most readily distinguish, but have been trimmed down for use on the web. This setting will produce images with the most accurate color.

We could choose the Web setting, which would be the most effective way to avoid dithering (a way of displaying colors not in the palette using a checkered pattern of two colors) but this will pump the file size up, which is something we're trying to avoid.

We're already using a No Dither setting, which means that if the color isn't in the palette, ImageReady will choose the closest match and use that, instead of a dither, to fake the color. The rest of the settings on the palette we won't fiddle with just yet.

6. Now have a look at the Color Table for this slice:

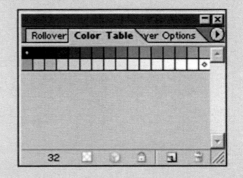

Where do all these colors come from? We talked earlier about using 6 colors to optimize this slice. There are only 4 colors in this slice, however. Or are there? Remember that the screen consists of lots of pixels – which are square in shape. Photoshop and ImageReady use a process of filling in colors to avoid having jagged diagonal lines, called anti-aliasing. These colors are called half tones, and are a combination of the line color and the background color. Let's take a close look at the tiny orange triangle in the bottom right hand corner of the slice:

11

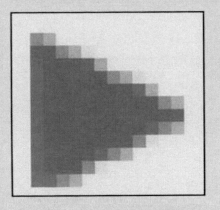

Notice how the diagonal edges of the triangle are comprised of colors which are a cross between the object (in orange) and the background (in cream).

> When you're adding transparency to an object Photoshop will ask you what color you wish to use as a matte. What this means is: Which color is going to be your background color? But if you're using transparency, you don't WANT a background right? As you can see in the above image, Photoshop still needs to know what the background color would have been, so that it can create all those half tones to ensure a non-jagged diagonal line.

So this is where all those extra colors are hiding! But as you can see, many of them are very similar. We can safely trim some of them down without losing too much image quality.

If we just use the tiny toggle arrows to the left of the 32 on the Optimize palette we can set how many colors should be used to display this slice. However, ImageReady will remove colors in its own way. What if we want to specify certain colors that should stay? For instance, if we remove all the orange colors, ImageReady will pick a black to display the arrow, which isn't acceptable. Luckily you can lock certain colors in place.

7. Click on a color in the palette or use the Eyedropper tool and click on the color on the actual slice. You can now use the tiny padlock icon at the bottom of the palette to lock this color. This means that no matter how many colors you

remove from the palette the locked color will be one of the remaining ones. In fact, let's lock four colors – the orange of the arrow, the black and white of the text and the cream/eggshell of the background:

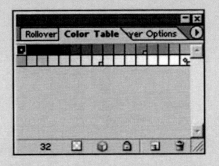

8. Now we can safely drop off as many colors as we please. We're basically going to drop off as many colors as we can, until ImageReady doesn't have enough to create a good enough anti-aliasing effect.

About 11 colors is all we need:

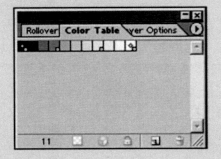

9. If we now use the 2-Up tab we can compare our optimized slice to the original:

1.268K for the slice, and we haven't lost any image quality! We could have obtained similar file size results using a JPG, but chances are we'd have found weird discoloration patterns creeping in – a side effect of how the JPG format optimizes. This isn't noticeable when we have lots of color variation, but it is very obvious with a flat color slice.

10. By optimizing each slice in this way, we can safely get the image down to around 18K. If we hadn't bothered with slices, but simply sacrificed file size, making the entire image 28K (a setting of around 5 using JPG file type) we would have horrible babble (areas of jumbled color) creeping into our image:

Clearly these areas needed to be optimized using the GIF format!

Adding a button

The last thing we want to do is to add a button action to the slice that has the text 'click here' on it. Let's make it so that when someone clicks on this particular slice, they go through to the catalog we created earlier.

1. Switch to the Slice Select tool (probably under the Slice tool).

2. Select the slice that you would like to become a button.

3. Using the Slice palette enter a URL into the field. Simple as that.

Background

1. We've designed our page to work in 800 by 600px. But what if people are in a larger resolution? Let's put a black background to the entire page using **File > Output Settings > Background** and choose black from the BG Color box. If the browser page is bigger than our design, this area will now be displayed as black.

2. Now we can save our web front-end using **File > Save Optimized As...**

ImageReady will now automatically create our hybrid image (which joins together all our different slices) and generate all the necessary HTML.

A final word

Whether you print out your photographs or display them on the web, Photoshop 7 should be an intrinsic part of the process. When you're up to your eyeballs in filters and layers, always remember to take a step back and look at the bigger picture. How is your final image going to look to other people?

It's great to match up colors so that they accurately display your original photograph. If your client is displaying the result in a neon lit factory however, you might need to take this environment into account. If your client is at the bottom of a mineshaft with a torch on his head, you're probably going to struggle...

Another important point is your audience's patience. By the time people browse to your website and look at your photographs, chances are their eyes are tired - they've probably been staring at their monitor for a while. Take their state of mind into account: Most people won't wait ages for huge file sizes to download. As not everyone has a wonderful 19-inch monitor to see the finer details of some of your images, it is better to offer an option of a higer quality version for those that want it, if they want it.

We've seen throughout this book how Photoshop can do things to your photographs – fix them, add to them, enhance them. Remember that time you used the wrong speed film, or you had the wrong aperture setting and you got this weird result? Pretty cool though wasn't it? Take this further with Photoshop. Try all sorts of filters out. Add lots of layers and mess with the blending modes. You never know what you might find...experimentation is the key to creativity.

11